ALL THAT YOU LEAVE BEHIND

All That You Leave Behind

A MEMOIR

Erin Lee Carr

BALLANTINE BOOKS
NEW YORK

Published in the United States by Ballantine Books,
an imprint of Random House, a division of Penguin
Random House LLC, New York.

BALLANTINE and the HOUSE colophon are registered
trademarks of Penguin Random House LLC.

LIBRARY OF CONGRESS CATALOGING-IN-PUBLICATION DATA
Names: Carr, Erin Lee, author.
Title: All that you leave behind: a memoir / Erin Lee Carr.
Description: First edition. | New York: Ballantine Books, [2019]
Identifiers: LCCN 2018059597| ISBN 9780399179716 (hardcover) |
ISBN 9780399178986 (ebook)
Subjects: LCSH: Carr, David, 1956–2015. | Carr, Erin Lee. |
Journalists—United States—Biography. | Recovering addicts—United
States—Biography. | Fathers and daughters—United States.
Classification: LCC HV5805.C356 A55 2019 | DDC 362.29/8092 [B]—dc23
LC record available at https://lccn.loc.gov/2018059597

Printed in the United States of America on acid-free paper

randomhousebooks.com

987654321

FIRST EDITION

Book design by Simon M. Sullivan

To my father, David Michael Carr, a ping-pong, dumpling, typing enthusiast who instilled curiosity in me above all else.

To my girl gang: Jill, Meagan, Madeline. Look how far we've come.

You know I'm not going to live forever. I won't be holed up in some hospital bed, dying slowly of lung cancer. You'll be the one to put the pillow over my face, right?

—DAVID CARR, DECEMBER 2014

AUTHOR'S NOTE

I know you know the drill but here it is: Some names and places have been changed to protect individual privacy. Memory is a fickle creature, but I have, to the best of my ability, remained true to the past, as it is available to me. The emails, Gchats, and texts are reminders of what happened and when. I am so grateful for their existence.

CONTENTS

ALL THAT YOU LEAVE BEHIND

The Blue House

When I think back to my early childhood home in Minneapolis, my brain conjures up a dim outline of a blue house on Pillsbury Avenue. While it is hard to remember the exact details of the house, the memories of its inhabitants come quite easily. I can picture my hands on the furniture, always trying to spread my mess out onto our sparse belongings. I see my dad putting one of our purple tutus on his head and declaring to no one in particular, "I am TUTU MONSTER," as he scoops my sister and me up in his arms while we shriek and try to scramble out of his grasp, giggling the whole time. He had a gift for creating worlds.

Our parents shape and create our reality. For a long time we have no sense outside of their worldview.

A while back I spent some serious time digitizing hundreds of decades-old photos tucked away in ancient red photo albums so that I could pull them up in a moment's notice. The images tell a familiar tale. Two little girls encased in baby buckets, looking up at the bad hair and fashions of the 1980s. Sometimes we are smiling in the photos. More often, though, we are not. We were born without so much as a wisp of hair, so naturally my grandma JoJo took to scotch-taping bows on our heads. She needed people to know that we were baby girls, not boys.

My mother is absent from these photos. It's just a flurry of aunts and uncles and Mountain Dew cans. My arms are chubby, and I am often reaching out for *more*. There is no baby book that recounts my first words or steps, but when I asked my dad in my teendom what my first utterance was, you better bet he said DaDa.

Meagan is so tiny in these early images, her body so small it looks like she could evaporate. Our nicknames mimic our stature; as luck would have it, I am known as Beefaroni and she, Noodles. I am often captured with a bottle in hand, and in a couple of photos, trying to grab the bottle from Meagan's hands.

There's one photo of my dad in these albums that I studied carefully. It's not like the others. He is in some sort of rec room, and he is standing up at a podium. He looks like he is clocking in around three hundred pounds, and he has a beard. Not exactly in fighting shape. Other men fill the room. He looks focused and nervous, photographed in midsentence.

I called Uncle Joe. He is warm and charismatic with a bald head and small circular glasses. I'd been remiss in calling. Life had gotten busy.

"Do you remember this photo?" I asked, after describing it to him. "What was he like then?"

Joe paused to think about it. I could tell that he was placating me. This was the second time in ten years he'd had to revisit a past that was very dark for his entire family. My dad spent some serious time excavating the facts of his life for his own memoir, *The Night of the Gun*. "Well, your dad was a mystery to us. He tried his hand at treatment on numerous occasions, and it just never seemed to stick. We knew—and I think he knew—that this time had to be different. Must have been at a meeting."

We were the stakes. These little babies needed a parent, and my mother was not going to magically reappear from Texas or

Mexico or wherever she was at that time. We needed him. "But didn't that intensify the pressure?" I asked.

"Well, didn't your dad always thrive under pressure?"

Why, yes, he did.

As Meagan and I age in the photos, our hair begins to grow and we go from looking like little old men to looking like little girls. Starting around age four, a soft white-and-pink checkered baby blanket starts appearing next to me, as if it were surgically attached. As I sought out other archival material from this time, I came across his column in the *Family Times*, a local paper that had given him some space to muse about life as a single dad. The column was aptly titled "Because I Said So." In one install-ment, he told of how he'd turned away for a second to look for my ever-quiet sister, and before he knew it I had gotten myself into our junker of a car and started backing out of the driveway. The minor heart attacks that surround the life of a young parent astound me.

In those early days in Minnesota we were poor. We needed government assistance just to get by—something I have no shame about and am frankly grateful existed at the time. You can tell our circumstances from the backgrounds in the photos, but you definitely wouldn't know it to look at Meagan or me. Grandma JoJo was a hawk at rummage sales and would find matching outfits (plus bonnets, no less) for us to wear for family photo ops. My dad, on the other hand, looks pretty ragged. I can see in his face that the financial fear was alive and well. He, alone, was responsible for these two little beings. Sure, his fam-ily could help here and there, but they needed their money to stay in their own pockets.

In the photos, he's always looking at us—his daughters. He isn't mugging for the camera, like he did in his early party-boy days. Instead, he is watchful, careful, and looks exhausted as hell. Someone caught him cracking a smile in one photo. We are at our grandparents' and Meagan and I are standing on top of the picnic table. There are garbage bags that hold something bulky underneath. We are told to open the bag and OH MY GOD we each have our very own tricycle to ride! The next photo is me on my trike, in my Easter bonnet, grinning from ear to ear. Dad watches us with parental glee but also relief: *Good, something to keep them busy.*

Having twin baby girls makes you value routine. Wake up, feed them, put them down for a nap, write until you hear the sound of a laugh or cry, and clumsily make your way toward the crib. Rinse, repeat. All noted in the journal he kept back then. One daily tradition that endured throughout our time together was the song before bedtime. He would come into our room—Meagan on top, me on the bottom of our wooden bunk beds—and read us a story. Inevitably we would beg for more. Just one more! He would shake his head and say, "How about a song?" Then he would launch into his simple tune:

Oh, I've got the nicest girls in town
Oh, I've got the nicest girls in town
They are so nice, they are so sweet, I love them twice, they
can't be beat
Oh,
I've
Got
The
NICEST girrrrrrllsssssss in townnnnnnnnn.

As a teenager I would roll my eyes when he would start in on this familiar refrain, but secretly I loved it. He would capitalize on the lore, at one point presenting both Meagan and me with a golden trophy, a gilded plaque that read NICEST GIRL IN TOWN. I wasn't sure if I deserved the award, but I accepted it willingly.

Memories of the softness and creativity of these moments warm me. They are evidence of his fierce love, devotion, and effort when it came to his girls. I know how rare it is to be so truly considered.

To: Erin Lee Carr, Meagan Marie Carr
From: David Carr
Date: 04/15/2014
Subject: a 26th birthday thought

My precious girls,

We are now at the part I had not anticipated, the part of being your parents when you are still becoming, but very much who you are.

If I say that I am proud of you, it somehow suggests that you are a reflection of my dreams. You are, but you are both so much more than that. I knew you were nice girls, good girls, but you have turned out in ways I would have never anticipated.

You guys are scary brilliant, ferocious and determined in both your intellectual life and matters of the heart. Yes, you are empathetic—I'm looking at you Meagan—and hilarious—put your hands in the air, Eronsky—but you are both deep thinkers, throbbing intellects that are always processing.

I can see each of you making significant contributions to not just our family or your respective communities, but the family of man. There is no limit on how far each of you will go. And I mean that. When you were growing up, I switched from wanting you to be mine to wanting you to be safe to wanting you to be comfortable to wanting you to be happy. Now, I want to watch you take over the world. Hyperbolic, to be sure, but every time I mix it up with you guys about significant matters, I come away smarter and questioning what I thought I already knew.

Erin: I have watched you in the middle of the city with a box of your office crap and alone in a room struggling to make beautiful important things. As someone who has seen a fair amount of talented young people up close, I can say that you are in the far reaches of that bunch. To call you a natural is to dismiss all the shit you ate to get where you are, but you instinctively understand the next right thing that brings you closer to the story you are trying to tell. You cannot teach that or inherit that or game that. That is you. That is who you have become. Your stories will be on the lips of not just your tribe, but many, many others.

Meagan: When you chose your path, I assigned it as a natural outgrowth of your journey. As it turns out, your intuition around humans—always a bit freaky to behold—is matched by an acute sense of intellectual inquiry. You are a scholar in all that entails and soon enough, a professional with a box of tools so big it will be hard to carry. Jesus, are you smart. You are always pulling back the blankets on what is in front of you, wanting to know why, wanting to know how, wanting to know more. In a family that doesn't do brilliant, you are threatening to change the game. You exist in a rarified cohort, and yet you still manage to stick out. We will, in the end, have a hard time getting to the end of all the things you know about humans and their behaviors.

Who knows where the drive at your level comes from? Both Jill and I have done our bit, working to make sure that our work is meaningful and sometimes remarkable, but that doesn't explain why each of you is working, striving, pushing to become something uncommon. There is, in both of you, an unwillingness to settle, a restlessness and frank ambition. Can you imagine how much joy that gives us as parents who have watched you grow up? Teeny, tiny little girls, afraid of toilets, or getting in trouble, or not having real friends, and now look at you. Life gives us things, amazing things, to stare at, but you are both the marvels of our life.

I find you both adorable, as I always have. We looked at the wedding album the other day and I was taken away by the trust and love you stared at us with. It made me happy that we have, in our bumpy ways, been worthy of that belief.

Please know that Jill and I are so glad that you have matured into re-markable young women with good values and standards that will serve you for the rest of your lives. But we are also aware that you have become creative forces and serious thinkers. We talk about you, marvel at you, speculate about your futures. We love being your parents, but we also like being your fellow travelers on this part of the road. Our amazement is less about the narrative of your conflicted birth, or complicated backstory, and more about what you have done as the ground turned solid beneath you. I look hard at the choices you have made since in terms of your health, your demons, and your challenges. You are tough young women who refuse to succumb when things are hard. You fight back.

We no longer pat your head, but wonder what else might be inside of them. I had no idea about this part, the part where you turn not only into adults, but big deals in your own right. We find it deeply exciting and can't wait to see the splendors and achievements still to come.

There is struggle now and you know what? There will always be struggle. As soon as you figure out the job, or the case, or the story, there will be another. The reward for achievement is a hunger for more, a blessing that lives inside a curse.

So why struggle? Why not the easier, softer way? Part of it comes from fear. Maybe we aren't all that. Maybe everyone who doubted us was right. But it goes beyond that.

We are workers, we are earners, we are strivers.

But still. We are not greedy people, we don't care for money except when we don't have any and we don't keep score by looking at or comparing ourselves with others.

Here's what I would say about rising above, being more, pushing for excellence. It is the way that life was meant to be lived. The joy of accomplishment, of making or doing something we are proud of, is something that endures in the end. I care less and less that others think I am a big deal and care more and more about what I think. Is what I did worthy of what I have been given? Am I getting in the boat and rowing, along with others, to the far shore of excellence?

It is a mystery why that matters to me, why it matters to Jill, why it matters so much to you both. But it is our way, it is how we roll and it's okay to own and revel in it.

But it is also deeply important that you come to rest on what you have accomplished and look behind you to see how far you have come. There is quiet, real happiness in that and it's the only way we find the strength and hope for the next climb. We are with you on every step, rooting you on and shaking the pompoms when things go your way.

We are so profoundly proud of you both.

Happy birthday to you, Noodles, and to you, Beefaroni. Who would have guessed it would turn out this way?

Dad

2

Rain Check

In January 2015, I got an email from my stepmom, Jill. The subject line read "Helping dad tomorrow morning." She told me that my dad was getting his pancreas "looked at" the next day around 7 A.M. at the hospital, and that she wanted me there as she had a pressing meeting at her office and couldn't stay to be the point person. I said yes immediately but felt uncomfortable. My dad had battled health issues for twenty years. He didn't like to involve his kids or cause them to worry unless it was absolutely necessary.

I got to the hospital and saw him standing outside smoking one of his Camel Lights, a lifelong habit. He seemed distracted. We went inside and sat in a cramped hospital waiting room while Jill stood at reception, filling out the paperwork and handing over the necessary ID and insurance cards. He told me he had an assignment for me while he was under. He had his Monday *New York Times* column already fleshed out; it was about the British television show *Black Mirror*.

"Please look this over and have thoughts for me when I come out," he instructed.

I nodded and whispered, "Good luck," and took a seat in the waiting room chairs. His giant backpack rested in the chair next to me, and I ran my hands up and down the mesh, trying to ground myself. Jill waved to me as she quickly exited and headed off to work. I was left alone with my thoughts—something I hated, especially in that moment.

I sat in limbo, surrounded by whitewashed walls covered in shitty generic artwork. I tried to read over his column, but my eyes couldn't focus, let alone my brain. It was after the holidays and my thank-you cards had not gone out. I'd bought some premade ones on Amazon that I had to fold to make usable—good manners, least labor intensive. The only task I could manage was to fold the blank cards in between touching his backpack, hoping it would provide me with some kind of comfort.

An hour later, as he lay in the recovery room, he sent me an email with the subject line "All good. Are you soon."

The "good" made me smile; the typo in the subject line made me laugh. I think he meant to say "See you soon." Perhaps "Are you coming soon?"

A half hour later, he smiled weakly as he walked over to retrieve me and his backpack.

"So what happened?" I asked.

"They thought there was a shadow on my pancreas, but it turned out to be nothing. So, lucky us. What did you think of the article?"

"I . . . I . . . thought it was great," I half-whispered. "I mean, I haven't seen the show."

He shook his head at me, disappointed that I hadn't been able to muster more of a response.

We walked over to a bagel store on Second Avenue. It was an old-fashioned joint with the menu spelled out in black type on a backlit yellow board. I nervously started to chatter on about nothing in particular, unable to withstand the silence.

We ate bagels with scallion cream cheese on plastic lunch

trays. I asked him about work. "We already talked about that," he reminded me.

I walked him to his car, which was parked in an underground lot nearby. He mentioned having advance screeners of an upcoming HBO show in an attempt to woo me back to the family home in New Jersey for some quality time. I shook my head and told him I would have to take a rain check. I had therapy and work and didn't want to make the trek back into the city later that day. I gave him a kiss goodbye and watched as he pulled out and headed home.

I had a couple of hours to kill before my appointment. I wandered into Sephora, not entirely sure why I had gone in as I didn't wear much makeup. A saleswoman came up to me. Did I need some help? Before I could stop myself I heard the words tumble out of my mouth: "Yes. I didn't really grow up with a mom, and so I've never really gotten the hang of doing any of this." My mom, a nearly lifelong addict, had never given up drugs long enough to be a part of my life. I'd never thought to ask my stepmom for help in this department, and she'd never offered.

The saleswoman took pity on me and started with a lesson on how to apply foundation. This temporary maternal substitute guided me toward the high-end stuff as a well-versed, commission-dependent surrogate mom might do, but I didn't even care. She took a cotton pad and started dabbing a little on my face and rubbing it in. I closed my eyes. I felt a little bit better. I looked in the mirror and saw dark circles under my eyes. "How can I hide these?" I asked.

I got to the checkout counter with a small assortment of potions. The total came to around seventy-five dollars. I fumbled inside my mesh messenger bag for a credit card, already feeling stupid for spending so much on stuff that I would never use.

• • •

Looking back, I play this day over and over in my mind: the fact that I chose to squander my free time in a makeup store, in search of a surrogate parent, when my actual parent had asked to spend time with me. The shadow on my dad's pancreas had rattled me deeply. I wish more than anything that I had known at that time what was to come.

3

The Night in Question

Sitting in the back of the cab, I was frantic. He had emailed me reminding me not to be late, and of course here I was, ten minutes behind schedule. The cab pulled up to the curb, and as I jumped out I felt the slap of cold air hit my face. The wind had been relentless that winter, and this night was no different. Inside, my dad was mediating a discussion with filmmaker Laura Poitras, journalist Glenn Greenwald, and former government contractor Edward Snowden (by way of Skype). They talked about making *Citizenfour*, a smart, intense documentary about the National Security Agency leaking scandal that unfolded in 2013, a call to arms regarding privacy in the United States. The panelists were thrilling to watch. I took notes; I always took notes at my dad's talks, as he expected a full report.

Afterward, we walked outside into the cold, and I waited for him to light a Camel. I noticed when he didn't, and he told me he'd been off cigarettes for four days, a herculean task for someone who'd been smoking one or two packs a day for some forty-odd years. Recently, he'd had a tough go of it—two bouts of pneumonia had left him running on empty. He'd decided cigarettes were the reason and quit once and for all. I considered asking him to dinner, but he said he was tired. He pulled my boyfriend Jasper in for a bear hug (we don't do handshakes in my family), and I hugged and kissed him goodbye before he headed back to the *Times* for his backpack. I felt the wool from his scarf scratching my neck as I leaned in to hold him close.

I walked with Jasper from the theater to a local dumpling shack, where we took refuge from the weather. Jasper was tall and angular with a quick and easy smile, and I realized I liked him, a lot. We chatted about conspiracy theories over scallion pancakes. We'd been dating for a little over a year. He'd been to many of my father's talks and enjoyed them.

"Did my dad seem okay?" I asked.

"Yeah, of course," said Jasper. "He was just tired."

It was Thursday night, and I had work to do at my office in Brooklyn the next day, so I kissed Jasper goodbye and headed into the subway. When I got out, I had two missed calls from Jill. I called her back.

"Listen to me carefully, and do not panic," she said. "Someone called me from the *Times* saying that Dad has collapsed. I need for you to get to St. Luke's Hospital. I'm in New Jersey and heading into the city right now, but you're closer and can get there first. I called Monie and she will be there to meet you. Do not call your sisters. I want to know what the situation is before I call them."

She hung up and I looked at the subway, calculating how long it would take to get to the hospital, before realizing that was insane and quickly hailing a cab. After I closed the car door, I sat and obsessed over the lack of descriptors in Jill's call. What did "collapsed" mean? Was he conscious? Alive? I called my best friend, Yunna. My voice cracked. She sounded startled by the news but told me everything was going to be okay.

"What if it isn't?" I whispered.

"It has to be," she said.

I listened to an audiobook on my iPad (his iPad that he gave me), anticipating that I'd need to be in a semi-stable state of mind for whatever came next. I played Gretchen Rubin's *The Happiness Project* and tried to stop sobbing. When I paid the fare, my cab driver mumbled, "I'm sorry." I nodded but had no words.

Monie, a close family friend, was there waiting. As I ran to her, she said loudly to the security officer in the triage area: "This is David Carr's daughter!" Just hours before, I had heard those words as I tried to find my seat at his event. My whole life it had been my introduction; I hoped to God that I would hear it again.

Dean Baquet, executive editor of *The New York Times,* walked over to me in the ER reception area. There was nothing to say except the truth: "He's gone. I'm so, so sorry." I heard shrieking; Monie was screaming loudly. I was mute. I noticed that Dean was wearing a purple scarf. Jill had not yet arrived.

They led Monie and me into a small waiting room where a young bearded guy was seated. Apparently he was the one who'd found my dad's unconscious body on the floor of the *Times* newsroom. He had tried to do CPR but was unsuccessful. He looked down. None of us had a single thing to say. Boxes of tissues littered the top of the generic wooden coffee tables. I reached for one.

I excused myself and went to the bathroom to call Jasper.

"Is he okay?"

I didn't yell or scream the worst words I have ever said out loud. Instead, I whispered them, willing them back into my head, but there they were.

"He died."

I threw up immediately.

"Oh my God, babe, oh my God," Jasper said over and over. His words rang in my ears.

I sat on the floor in the hospital bathroom trying to compose myself. An impossible task. I started a mental Rolodex, automatically flipping through all of the things my dad would not be around for.

My twenty-seventh birthday
My first film premiering at the Tribeca Film Festival in two
    months
Walking me down the aisle
The career we'd cleverly plotted together

One by one these thoughts crushed me and my vision of the future.

But then I realized my mental Rolodex was missing something important. What about him? His dreams, his goals? So much grander than my own.

Growing old together with the love of his life, Jill
Seeing my baby sister, Madeline, graduate from college
Seeing my twin, Meagan, graduate from her PhD program
Publishing his next book
Teaching another class at Boston University
Achieving his private, long-sought-after goal—a Pulitzer

What happens to all of these dreams when someone dies?

I asked Jasper to come to the hospital before he could even offer. I needed his body next to mine. Everyone was silent when I walked back into the waiting room, looking for Jill. When she appeared, our faces gave it away. She immediately looked down. She reached for no one as there was no solace to be had.

A doctor asked if we wanted last rites performed. We did.

Dad's editor Bill Brink was there to say the *Times* would be putting out a statement.

"But I have to call Meagan and Madeline and David's family," Jill said quickly.

"Can you do it now?"

I glanced down at my phone and found a text message from a former co-worker: "Hey, heard some scary news about your dad. I hope it isn't true." How did he know? Why is he texting me? I barely know him.

Apparently during the franticness of the moments between my dad's collapse and the medics arriving, a reporter at the *Times* tweeted that my dad had been found unconscious; she'd assumed the news was already public. Twitter had been notified.

And there it was. My first feeling that shattered the shock. Anger. Raw, seething, all-encompassing anger. *What the fuck. I haven't even seen my dad's body and already people are sending me texts like this.* I considered smashing my phone on the ground.

But there was no time for acting out; I had to go in and see my dad. Jill and I followed the doctor into the room where his body lay. His mouth and eyes were open, as if he were in mid-thought, about to say something. It was horrifying. Jill broke the silence: "Oh, sweeto, what happened?" She wrapped her arms around him and sobbed and then backed away, unable to hold on. I lay my head on his chest, but it didn't feel like him. His body was stiff and foreign. Jill and I held hands and said a prayer.

A hospital worker came in and informed us that the priest was running late and they would have to move "him" to free up the emergency trauma room.

Meanwhile, we needed to let our family know, and fast, before the *Times* released their announcement. The raw anger returned. Couldn't I have at least thirty seconds to comprehend what had happened before the Internet chimed in?

Helplessness is a savage feeling on a night like this. There were so many "jobs" to do, and yet I could barely summon the strength to call my twin. She picked up on the third ring. I was at a loss for words, so I opened with the cliché that the movies have ingrained in me: "I need for you to sit down."

"No," she answered. "Tell me what's wrong."

"I am at the hospital and there was an accident. Dad passed away."

Her shrieks pounded against my ears. I didn't know what else to call it other than an accident because to me, it felt like one, a terrible accident. No one just drops dead.

The New York Times sent out an alert; NPR did the same. His death trended on Twitter. The floodgates opened. I was split down my center by hundreds of texts, emails, and voicemails. It was beyond intrusive, and forced me to dissociate. Every minute my phone buzzed, and I would look down to see if it was a call I needed to take. All of the people finding out my dad was dead from a notification on their phone.

Some of my close friends showed up at the hospital and helped us back to Monie's house. Wine was uncorked, and slowly the shock became grief. Two months before I had secretly started drinking again after a nine-month stint of abstinence. I felt an unabashed need to drink my way through both what I'd just witnessed, and whatever came next. No one noticed. Or at least they didn't say anything. It was not the time for reprimands.

My stepmom, one of the strongest, most stoic women I know, began to cry out over and over again for my dad, her partner of more than two decades. We sat with her. There was nothing else we could do. We talked about the day that had just transpired, hoping that retracing every single one of his steps could provide clues, but we found nothing solid.

Jasper and I spent the night at Monie's. He held me as I cried myself to sleep. I didn't have the energy or inclination to take off my clothes. They were what I was wearing when I hugged my dad for the last time.

I woke up the next morning certain that I was dying, too. The words "My dad is dead" beat like an awful drum inside my head.

Suddenly, a memory flashed. Christmas Eve, a few weeks before. We were all sitting around the living room. My dad had made a point to celebrate how life had worked out nearly perfectly for everyone in our family. Relationships, jobs, money, happiness. I remember thinking how right he was. "Everything has broken our way," he'd concluded.

Now everything was just broken.

4

The Ghost in You

My dad's doctor called. It hadn't even been a day since he'd died. Talking to the doctor seemed a little beside the point to me, but Meagan wanted answers. She'd emailed the good doctor to see if there was any sort of explanation behind our father's unexpected death. I had Dr. Keen's number in my phone from years past. I picked up immediately when she called, and she softly stated the obligatory words of condolence. I hit speakerphone and introduced Meagan as the brains of the operation.

My sister paced back and forth in the family dining room as she began the inquiry. I am sure the doc was nervous; she was my dad's primary care physician, and he had seen her repeatedly in the last six months. It seemed like he was always headed to or from her office whenever we spoke. There were warning signs. His appearance had changed. He had lost his appetite and a fair amount of weight; he had frequent bouts of pneumonia; and his stamina, forever a staple in his life, was beginning to wane. They had been searching for a reason for his weight loss.

The shadow over his pancreas? The scan came back clean. His diabetes was acting up, but that could have been due to any number of reasons. His smoking was always a problem, but there was nothing anyone could do about that.

Meagan had a simple question: "What did he die of?" Dr. Keen was very careful and measured in her response. She told us that we would have to wait for the official autopsy report, but early signs looked like lung cancer. The scans he'd had just weeks before hadn't yet revealed the mass on his lungs. He'd had a chest X-ray, but apparently it didn't extend far enough, and they had missed it. My dad had an appointment with a pulmonologist scheduled for the week after he died. The doctor contended that they likely would have found the tumor then. The call solidified what we already knew—that he did not know he was dying.

Meagan hung up the phone. Then, after a long pause, she said, "Okay, so that's good. He didn't know."

"Yeah, what a relief," I said sarcastically. I knew the quest for information was an important one, but my fuse was short. Just about everything in the world made me angry at this point.

Right now, Jill was quiet and focused as she concentrated on the task ahead of her. She carefully arranged the hospital and insurance papers on the dining room table, which is what they used to do with their bills. She called my dad's credit card companies and gave them our bad news. There were piles of newspapers stacked up at the house; he read four papers a day. How was he able to get through that amount of information in one day? No one had thought to cancel any of the subscriptions yet. I watched her silently as she went about the business of dealing with death.

She glanced up and said, "We still have a couple of things that we have to do today. Someone has to go identify the body." I found myself volunteering for the job. I'd do anything to get outside the claustrophobic house.

"Are you sure?" Jill asked. The image of my father's dead body at the hospital would never leave my skull. I could at least spare my sisters the same assault.

A few hours passed, and I began to lose my nerve. I started to panic about walking into the morgue alone. Jasper sat in the living room with his head down. He had been a staple around the house but was ever mindful of fading into the background. I asked him what book he was reading, and he told me it wasn't important. No other information really matters in the days after a death. I think he knew what was about to come next. I asked if he would drive me into the city and help me identify the body. I couldn't do it alone. He said of course, though I could sense he was deeply uncomfortable.

As I got into Jasper's car I patted myself down for my phone, knowing I'd be unable to do anything without it. Unlike at the hospital, today the phone felt like armor, with its constant buzzing as friends and acquaintances reached out to tell me how much my dad meant to them. It felt like a slot machine; every time I unlocked it I got a small dose of dopamine. It was one of the only things keeping me intact. I was opting out of the present in favor of a digital realm where I didn't have to call the doctor or figure out what I needed for the morgue. I could just be comforted.

We typed "NYC morgue" into Google Maps and I stifled a small laugh—how comedically awful our lives had become in a single day. We put on a Spotify playlist of my dad's favorite songs, of which there were thousands. The day before, Jasper and I had shortened it to those we could remember: fifty-six songs, three hours and forty-five minutes' worth.

"The Ghost in You" by Robyn Hitchcock hummed through the speakers.

Inside you the time moves and she don't fade
The ghost in you, she don't fade

He'd sent me the song eleven days before he died when he'd requested my presence at the family home in New Jersey for the

Super Bowl. I had spaced and wound up without wheels that day. He told me he would pay for half of a Zipcar, but it was just important that I get there and soon. When I told him we were en route, he'd attached the song to his return email, writing "Great. Please put this on in the car."

I cursed myself as we made our way to the morgue. As if on cue, a tear leaked out of my eye as we rolled up to East Twenty-sixth Street to what seemed to me to be one of the sadder buildings in New York: a block-long behemoth with a sign out front that reads OFFICE OF CHIEF MEDICAL EXAMINER.

I crept up to the front desk and saw a clipboard. Instinctively, I knew that I wouldn't need to talk if I just filled out the attached form. My dad's body was in this building. I wondered if I'd be looking at an image of him or his actual body. I filled out his date of birth, and felt like screaming when I did the math.

58.

58.

58.

Who dies that young? No one had ever prepared me for his dying that young.

I turned in the clipboard. I sat and stared at my shoes, cheap black boots against the beige linoleum, caked with dirt. I hugged myself with my arms and closed my eyes. When I looked up, I saw people in the same zombified state. The morgue is not a place you want to spend your Saturday.

After five long minutes, they called my name, and I was led by an administrator into a small room with a computer screen. A woman seated behind a wooden desk asked me several questions, and I was completely mystified as to how someone could perform this job day after day. "How are you today?" "How do you know the deceased?" My mind trailed off thinking about it until she asked if I was ready. *This is it. I will see him for one last time on this screen.* Jasper reached for my hand and squeezed it.

"I guess." She swiveled the monitor toward me and asked me if this was David Carr, my dad and relative. I cried first and then nodded. He was on a metal gurney with a white sheet draped over the lower half of his body. His face, ever the same, was his, but lifeless. His mouth was still open.

"Yes, that's him," I told her, and with that, the business was done.

5

It All Starts Somewhere

"You are a Carr, and that is a complicated, wondrous inheritance."

No one gets to choose the traits they inherit from their parents. I was blessed with a semblance of smarts, blue eyes, and giant, man-sized feet. When I was thirteen, a kind, elderly pediatrician remarked that with feet like these, I was sure to grow in height.

At twenty-seven years old I'm still five feet, four inches. But other promised inheritances have come true. Some darker than others, like a fondness for the drink.

When I was growing up, my dad often whispered to us, "Everything good started with you." I realized the converse truth—that there must've been an "everything bad" before there was an everything good.

When I was in third grade, living in Washington, D.C., a friend came over after school one day. Let me preface this by saying this wasn't a typical event in my life. I was an awkward kid who had no clue as to what was "cool," and the savvy kids knew to stay the hell away from me. Finally, after many failed attempts, I made a friend. Her name was Alex.

Jill picked us up from school, and I remember Alex gave me a funny look when I called Jill by her first name, instead of "Mom," and later asked me about it when we were alone in my room. I explained to her what had been explained to me, that my parents used to be drug addicts, but my dad no longer did drugs and was now married to Jill. You know, basic eight-year-old stuff.

A couple of hours later, my dad popped his head in and asked: "Do you girls want to go to McDonald's?"

"Yesssss," we screamed automatically. We ambled toward our family's junky Ford Explorer, and when Alex could see that it would just be my dad, the two of us, and my sister, she crossed her arms and refused to get in.

"Do you need help getting in?" my dad asked patiently.

Alex shook her head, then stated matter-of-factly, "I am *not* getting in the car with a drug person."

The words stung my ears, and my heart quickened in a frightening way. Without missing a beat my dad quietly replied, "Well, then, I guess we won't be going." Within an hour, Alex was gone, picked up and driven away by her mom, who was not a drug person. I sat in my room, upset that my first real playdate was such a failure.

I heard my dad bellow from downstairs: *"Erin, get down here!"* He motioned for me to sit down on the maroon couch where Meagan was already seated, looking confused. He told us it was time to discuss our story and how to tell it. First of all, it was not information to be traded for affection. My dad carefully explained what drugs were, and why, in the past, he had used them. He reiterated that he was sober now and would remain so as long as he went to his "meetings." I asked him why our mom, who had exited our lives years earlier, wasn't sober. He looked at Jill, unsure what to say.

It was hard for my eight-year-old brain to grasp the true dark story of what had happened, but I eventually learned that my parents' appetite for cocaine was monstrous, quickly moving from recreational use into freebasing, all on top of their regular abuse of alcohol. A toxic mix. No one celebrated when my mom found out she was pregnant, but the show went on. My mother claims she used only a couple of times while we were in utero, though she is the only one who knows this for sure. After six and a half months of pregnancy, her water broke and she went into labor. It was the spring of 1988, and the math did not look good.

Our premature little bodies were placed in incubators. I imagine the hospital staff just looked the other way when my parents came to visit. What to say? My dad and mom continued to use, and the relationship dissolved when the coke business was done. We were a product of the union but also a reminder that they were not good together; they split after we were born.

I have been told that my dad's moment of reckoning, as captured in his memoir, came when he left us in the dead of winter, strapped into our snowsuits in the car, to go score and get high in a nearby crack house. We could have frozen to death.

In our first year he and my mom took turns taking care of us, these little babies. She had two previous kids of her own, and it was obviously a lot to handle. Once again she turned to drugs. It was clear that she was not a viable option in terms of guardianship, nor was my dad. Who was left?

In December 1988, when we were eight months old, my dad entered an inpatient rehabilitation facility whose name was held in a sort of reverence in our home: Eden House. My sister and I were placed temporarily in foster care through Catholic Charities. Our caretakers were Zelda and Bob, kind Minnesotans whose kids were all grown up. When my dad was writing *The Night of the Gun,* he interviewed them, and they recounted his erratic behavior. Direct, intense, falling over. He wanted us to receive perfect care, but he looked desperately unable to provide any. Zelda recalled feeling horrified and glad to scoop us up into her arms. My grandmother was with him when he dropped us off. She didn't have high hopes. It would be his fifth time in treatment.

My dad was the fourth of seven kids. He outlived both of his parents, John and Joan Carr, but barely. His dad was a smart, well-dressed Minnesotan with a fondness for speaking in his own homegrown idioms. His mom, Joan, whom we called JoJo for short, was a loud, friendly, loving creature who became deeply involved in Catholic Charities and the local St. Patrick's Day parade. I'm told that my dad was a wryly funny kid, a voracious reader, and very much a middle child. His brothers picked on him, but challenged anyone that tried to do the same at school. He loved mischief and would try to get away with as much trouble as possible.

After much hard work on his part, we were returned to our dad after he successfully finished his six-month program. He had the reason for recovery right there in front of him. What would happen to us if he picked up a drink or used again? I can only imagine how unmanageable it must have felt for him at times, single-parenting two babies that needed every goddamn thing from you.

When we were growing up, my dad spoke to us often about the joy and terror that took hold in those years. He made sure to show us the finer places in town, even though we had very little money. That meant the lunch special at the local Vietnamese restaurant known to us as Quang Deli. Giant, steaming bowls of pho soup would arrive at our table. The cilantro, onions, and beef swirled around to create a magnificent concoction. We were taught to use chopsticks from the earliest of ages, no forks for these kids. The waiters smiled at what must have been an odd sight, this large bearded man accompanied by two animated cherubs. My dad would lean in close to us and whisper before motioning to our waiter. When he approached the table,

Meagan or I (let's be real, mainly me) would pipe up and say, "More meat please!" What a con artist, using a baby to get some free grub. He played the game well.

We developed a life, in small, finite ways. Grocery store, walk home, dinner, bath, story, bed. A routine is what we all craved after the chaos early on. His lawyer Barbara asked him to keep a journal of our life together, in case the judge needed proof that he knew what he was doing. How many times he changed us, what he fed us, what bedtime looked like. While the diary started off as the ramblings of an incoherent and sleep-deprived addict in early recovery, it became the written testament of a single parent who fiercely loved his children. And we loved him back.

Oct. 1, 1990

It is a Fall monday and they both are as sweet as only little girls can be, different as only sisters can be. We spend the quickly darkening fall evening wheeling up and down on your plastic trikes—one purple and one red.

Erin knows how to work the pedals as she rolls by, pointing to her feet and saying "Watch." I sit on the steps and listen to the chatter. "My bike. Two bikes." Erin talks constantly. "No touch," she says, wagging a finger at me.

Meagan is less specifically interested in riding, unless she gets some distance between me and her. As soon as I yell and begin to run after, she goes like the wind in the other direction. A white kitty stalks both girls as they ride.

Both girls insist on a bath when we get upstairs, bolting naked as soon as their clothes are removed. Long peals of laughter trail behind them like vapor, hovering even as the bare footfalls fade.

Right this minute, the girls are playing a game of their in-

vention in the tub. Like so many others, it involves one accomplishing some little task and the other cheering like there's no tomorrow when it is accomplished. They take turns . . . mostly.

It's near 8 and they will soon both be in bed and I will be grateful. Grateful they are mine, grateful they are so precious, and very grateful they are finally out of my hair. bye for now.

Jill came into our lives in 1994. She was blond, stylish, and basically my dad's exact opposite. Her beauty was outmatched only by her smarts, and he was instantly smitten. Jill was a former director of administration for the Republican National Convention and in 1994 was headed back to her home state of Minnesota to apply to grad school to become a teacher. They met at a bar at a gathering of mutual friends. Sarah, a woman my dad had waited tables with, thought they might hit it off and had invited them both out. True to knucklehead form, my dad brought a date with him. When Sarah walked over to make the introduction, she sized up my dad's date and said he should come over solo. My dad rolled his eyes but followed her. He walked into the next room and there was Jill. They shook hands and everything melted away. He asked her out immediately. True, she did not resemble the women he had dated in the past—often brunette and a bit rough around the edges—but he had a feeling that Jill was something else, something quite singular.

Our dad made it clear to Meagan and me that Jill was not a replacement for our mother. As a six-year-old, I didn't know quite what to make of her. Upon our initial meeting I eyed her curiously. I knew what "girlfriend" meant—that they liked each other. I liked her short, blunt blond bob and her smile. I liked the fact that she had a goofy chocolate-colored dog that she named Eileen because the dog, well, leaned. But I sometimes found our interactions with her confusing. She didn't hug or cuddle us the way Grandma or Dad did. Instead, she waited for us to come to her.

They married quickly; he proposed on Christmas Eve—they hadn't even been dating a year. He knew he had a good thing. Their parents threw a boisterous, loud wedding. Meagan and I were appointed flower girls and wore petite white dresses with flat-brimmed hats. The wedding photos elicit a type of fairy-tale narrative. I don't remember feeling scared about my family changing; I was just happy to have an occasion where I could eat multiple pieces of cake.

In September 1995, a year after they got married, we moved from Minnesota to Washington, D.C., where my dad had accepted a job working as an editor for the respected alternative weekly *Washington City Paper*. Jill was pregnant and less than thrilled to be moving so far away from her mom and family. But my dad had a mission and that involved being in D.C. She trusted him. So away we went.

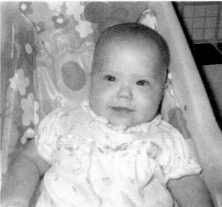

Dad nicknamed me Beefaroni. You might be able to see why.

Meagan, angelic in comparison to me, sleeping in her baby bucket.

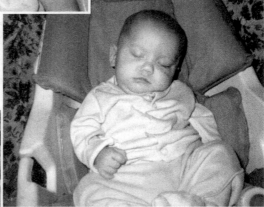

Grandma JoJo made us wear bonnets on a daily basis.

*We were nothing if
not fashionable.*

*We made the perfect eighties
trio. Dad was the drummer.*

Jill joins the gang.

6

The Other Woman

There was, of course, another woman in my dad's life—one who came before Jill. My mother, Anna.

Our relationship is a painful topic to think about, and I try to avoid it. I know that she wasn't dealt the best hand in life. Her own mother had her when she was forty and was worn out by the time my mom came along. My mom told me in a Facebook message (one of the few ways we currently communicate) that her mother was a quiet person who taught herself to paint. Her father was an alcoholic, and my mother was scared to death of him. He spent the last twenty years of his life a sober man and she grew to love him, but she never forgot who he used to be. Her brother fought in Vietnam and came back different. She told me he had major PTSD, and no one said anything about it; you didn't back then. His parents buried him in his mid-fifties. My mother moved away as soon as she could to start her own life, dreaming of love, if not wealth. She would find something else entirely.

When I look at photos of my mom, I search for the woman my dad fell in love with. She already had kids of her own when my father introduced her to smoking crack. He could be violent with her, and there were things that happened during their time together that she could not forgive. She's told me she feared for her life, but my dad said she left us with him to pursue her drug habit. He eventually filed for sole custody, citing child abandonment. There is no record of her contesting the paperwork or responding in any way. My dad became our sole guardian, a rarity back then for a father in child custody disputes.

I know I am like my dad in a variety of ways. But what about her? I am short, like her. Funny, caustic, same smile. I am a hustler just like she is.

While he raised and cared for us, he still wanted us to know our mother as we grew up. Her financial situation changed as often as her phone number (it's never the same; when I want to reach her I have to scroll through a long series of missed calls), and she usually asked my father for the money to send us to see her. We'd spend five days in the Arizona or Mexico heat living in her double-wide trailer, its chrome gleaming in the sun. I would devour books in the shade while my sisters frolicked in the ocean. It was a simple time, but the darkness of her life leaked out at the edges. Even as a child, I knew something was off. A boyfriend who shouted, money that vanished, the dog eaten by the local band of coyotes. The time she fell asleep and burned me with her cigarette. I was ten years old.

When I was in high school, my mother, while high on Percocet, hit and killed a man with her car. She had serious back problems her entire adult life and chewed on the pills to ease the pain. She was charged with vehicular manslaughter and sent to the local jail. She wrote me long letters in her beautiful script. I can't remember if I ever answered them. I have not seen her since I was fourteen years old.

My dad encouraged me to be tender toward this woman. I had a hard time with that. I didn't want to keep punishing her for choices she made decades ago, but what had she done for me besides give me life?

Racism, drug addiction, and mental illness were regular parts of the ongoing discussion my father had with us when we were growing up. He didn't hide the truth or even shrink it to kid-sized bits of information. If anything, he shared too much about the darkness of the world too early, hence my fuck-up with my little friend who refused to ride in the car with him. He told us we had to be careful about who we told our story to, but he wouldn't let us hide from it ourselves.

After all the stories, with all their hints of what I'd inherited, of course I would stay away from drugs. I was smart enough to avoid repeating the same mistakes. That path had been worn out, and I was going on the straight and narrow. Or so I believed.

7

Rites of Passage

After a stint in D.C., my dad accepted his dream job at *The New York Times*. Over the course of fifteen years, he had gone from editing at the *Twin Cities Reader* to working on the film, culture, and media beat at one of the most esteemed newspapers in the world. He had arrived. I, in turn, was attending a tiny, all-girls Catholic high school outside of New York City, pulling okay grades, and spending most weekends loading up on Monster energy drinks while watching *Dawson's Creek*.

During the summer of my sophomore year of high school, my friend Jenny and I invited our small cohort over to watch Ryan Phillippe bamboozle the ingénue Reese Witherspoon in *Cruel Intentions*. Buzzed on the underlying sexual tension, we were looking for something to do next.

"I know my parents keep a bottle of vodka around here somewhere, we could take turns," Jenny offered as she left the room in search of a bottle of lemon-flavored Ketel One. She came back with a bottle, and we traded swigs, all the while grimacing at how "gross" it tasted.

But in truth, it didn't taste gross to me; it tasted like pure magic. My head started to hum, my smile felt easier. The night devolved into YouTube videos and fits of laughter until we all passed out. Later that night, I stole to the basement one more time to take additional swigs. I pressed the bottle to my mouth until it was empty and promptly threw up all over the basement floor. The next morning, Jenny wondered aloud why I got so sick when we only had a couple of sips. I didn't have the courage to admit that I drank more by myself. Instinctively I knew that was something that should be kept secret.

The remainder of high school passed without further incident, as far as drinking went. I drank on a few occasions, but I never reached the stupor of that first time. While it held some allure for me, I was able to keep my desire for alcohol at bay, for the most part.

Eventually it came time for me to pursue higher education. Almost a decade after we left the Midwest, my family and I made the drive back—this time from New Jersey to Madison, Wisconsin, where I would be attending college. We pulled up in our Ford Explorer to the dorm that would be my home for freshman year; I was sweaty from days in the car with my dad, Jill, and Meagan. I was also sweaty from nerves. Did I look the part of a hip but edgy college freshman? I had dyed my hair an auspicious color of fire-engine red and cut it short. I rocked a Rolling Stones T-shirt and red-and-black-striped skinny jeans from the cult-kid-wannabe chain store Hot Topic. Years later, my dad teased me that it seemed like my mission was to go to college as ugly as possible.

Before he left me at the dorm he told me to have fun but to practice caution; he knew that college would be a time of high jinks. And as always he told me how desperately proud he was of me. A couple of tears leaked out of my eyes as he hugged me. I was ready, but that didn't mean it didn't hurt to say goodbye.

It took a while, but I started to get the hang of the whole college thing. I logged some serious time in the library, but I also devoted quite a few hours to drinking amber liquids at the famed Wisconsin student union with my beloved gang of miscreants. I felt like I found my people in college—weirdos like me who laughed loudly and stood out among the preppie Wisconsinites that lived for football Saturdays. Sure, we went to football games, but it was mostly just an excuse to drink.

Once, on a night before my dad was due to arrive for one of our biannual visits, my roommate Jamie clumsily elbowed me in the face while drinking. As a result, my Monroe piercing (a stud above the lip) became infected. It. Was. Not. Pretty.

When my dad stepped off the plane the next day, he took one look at me and said, "What the fuck?" It looked like someone had punched me in the mouth with a fake-diamond nail.

Instead of dropping off his luggage at the Best Western downtown, we headed straight for the piercing place on State Street. The Monroe had to go. I protested, albeit weakly, because in truth the throbbing in my face was getting to me. I kept my head down as we sat in the waiting room. My dad jumped on his phone and paced around, not paying his surroundings much mind. A cute guy with gauges called me over, and I reluctantly identified the man with me as my father. My dad made some deeply inappropriate joke about my roommate knocking me around as, in one swift motion, the cute guy removed my piercing.

Afterward, my dad told me he needed ten minutes to make another phone call. We walked outside. "What is it about you that trouble just sort of follows you around?" he asked, his expression one of bewilderment tinged with disappointment as he ducked away to make his call. When he was done, he walked back over to me on the sidewalk. I expected him to crack wise but was met with silence. He looked at me and said, "I have to say I am a little worried about you. . . . Did this happen while you were drinking?"

The question hung in the air. While my dad had been sober for most of my childhood, my mom had not. I knew what addiction looked like. The disorder ran in my genes. I tried to push that feeling to the far reaches of my brain whenever it surfaced, with moderate success, but I saw the disease infect the people in my life. Some would recover. Others, like my mother, would not. The warning was there when I took my first drink.

In college, I kept an online journal, and I typed furiously about my burgeoning drinking problem. Still, I got mostly Bs and some As. I could study and hold down a part-time job. I had a friend group that was full of smart, genuine people. I was responsible and showed up on time. But I often woke up drenched in sweat, paranoid about the things I did or said the night before, knowing I would just do it again the next weekend. Drinking, even when I was eighteen, started to guide my choices.

Still, I didn't want my dad to worry about me, and I definitely didn't want him to be disappointed. We wound up making a bet. The bet was really more of a bribe. He told me he would give me sixty dollars if I refrained from getting another piercing for one calendar year. I won the bet, begrudgingly. I needed the money.

On April 15, 2008, I finally turned twenty-one. My dad sent me a bottle of Dom Pérignon and a letter. Despite his misgivings about my drinking, he felt I deserved to enjoy some nice champagne. I never asked him why.

> *Dolly, do you have an idea how much I adore you and think of you?*
> *You are a fundamental joy of my life. Who you are and how you proceed brings me a sense of deep happiness I can't express in words.*

There is so much to like about who you are becoming that it
makes a very long list but let me just flick at a few things.
You are beyond question cool
You are smart and getting smarter
You are afraid of very few things
You are increasingly kind
You care about the world
You knew who Obama was before others did
You have a magnificent taste in music and film and the ability
to articulate your choices
You are a snot about culture, but not snotty
You are a Smith house fellow
You have matched wits with a meth head fry cook
You once had a nail sticking out of your face and were able to
act like it was nothing
You are a good sister, daughter, and friend
You are beautiful and have inimitable style
You are very flexible when it comes to hair color
You love your dad and he loves you back
Roar, Fahja

8

How (Not) to Intern

"Don't be scared. Be very happy.
This is the sound of yer life beginning. F."

In 2009, no one in America was immune to the ongoing global financial crisis, including the Carr household. I knew I had to get a job to help pay my college tuition. This was nothing new—I'd worked since I was fifteen. There was, however, the issue of what the hell I was going to do exactly in the real world with the communication arts degree that I was working toward. Maybe it was time for a summer internship, preferably one that paid, as I needed to eat.

Little did I know my dad was plotting something to help me gain entrance into the workforce. Late one Saturday night he sent me this email:

Erin, you know what? screw the economy. I think we can get something rolling for you seeing as you demonstrated early and specific interest. and you should know that part of the reason that i can recommend you without hesitation is the big leap you took in terms of responsibility and skill set this year as an RA. you should be proud of what you have already accomplished.

I need a bright, breezily written couple graphs about you and your experience. worked since x years old, waited tables, bartended, day-

care provider, and now assistant at campus media center and resi-
dent advisor . . . blah, blah, areas of study and interest, skills . . . html,
vid stuff, computer, etc. self describe as earner, worker, low maintenance, high reward, highly adaptable, having lived and worked in a
variety of environments and cities. from ordering food from meth
head fry cook upstate to negotiating peace between cops and resi-
dents in madison . . . mebee not quite that colorful, but something
like that.

and then statement of interests . . . all forms of pop culture, esp film,
television and music. etc. and then say what you are looking for . . .
internship . . . and what you are willing to do for it . . . basically anything. send that to me and I will start retailing it around on email to
people who might be interested. and I want a current photo emailed
under sep. cover.

let's get this train rolling.

xo, fahja

He had a sizable Rolodex filled to the brim with people I read
about regularly in my battered copies of *Entertainment Weekly.*
He liked to name-drop, and I was one of the only people in our
family who knew even the more obscure people he referred to,
so he was always eager to jump on the phone with me and talk
over the latest adventure or mishap on some red carpet and to
dish about who was mean and who was nice—or at least nice-
looking up close.

He'd requested a photo for the internship pitch, so I looked
over the few I had at my disposal (this was before the ubiquity
of the iPhone), taken recently on my cheap digital camera to
celebrate the one time I'd achieved the perfect liquid line on my
eye. It was an odd photo to send to your dad—or to a potential
employer—a selfie before they were a thing. I'm seated on a

couch; the top of my white T-shirt is somewhat in frame but it is mostly me glaring into the camera with my mouth slightly open and my eyes wide. My blond hair is swept to the side, late-aughts emo style, and I'm looking down into the camera. This is the photo I chose to say "Hey, give me a job! I'll try not to be annoying!"

Very professional photo to send to future employers, taken in my dorm room.

The following is what I drafted and sent to my dad:

The name is Erin Carr and I am graduating college and am desperately trying to avoid *The Graduate* type of situation because one, I don't own a deep-sea diving suit and two, I don't know anyone named Mrs. Robinson. I will ultimately graduate with a degree in Communication Arts from University of Wisconsin-Madison. I have worked at a variety of jobs including dancing to the oldies while making a mean banana split, educating the future of America at a learning center, pouring glass after glass of Glenlivet to old men who always have stories to tell (whether I want to hear them or not) and my one true passion: media. Media has fascinated me since my single digits up until now. While my peers were watching crappy teen soaps I was consuming all forms of media new and old, television and film, blogging, viding and capturing images compulsively. I understand that I am one of many that will attempt to work for you this upcoming summer but I am a girl who can lift things 1.5 my weight, break down a set, make problems disappear and take enormous pride in doing small things well while taking an interest and sometimes helping with bigger things. Please contact me if you have any room available on your team, I would love to work for you.

I also added to the email: "Where do I put in that I am your daughter, and is there a classy way to do that?"

He read the pitch and told me it needed to be shorter and funnier (a good rule of thumb for most things). He then sent me back the following revision:

My name is Erin Carr and I will be a senior at University of Wisconsin-Madison next year. I want to be part of your production/caper as a go-fer/gaffer/girl-friday. I'm working hard to find an internship in the media/movie world for this summer. So far I've done a lot of simple but hard jobs and done well. If you're learning disabled, I worked as a coach at a learning center. If you're hungry, I've waited more tables than I care to remember. If you enjoy a cocktail, I know what an Old Fashioned is and how to make it.

More to the point, I currently handle a variety of media and formats at the Instructional Media Development Center and also rule 40 freshmen in a dorm with a not-so iron fist. I am in the midst of assisting in the camerawork for a project about the classification of dairy cows. (Guernsey's rock, btw) I am still a hack with Final Cut Pro, but improving daily. I have deep love and growing knowledge of independent cinema and sprawling tastes in all kinds of music. I am the most mediated person I know with an external hard drive filled with gigabytes of film, music, and text. My internal hard drive, my brain, is in a nascent state and seeking new experiences and lessons from the likes of you. I am a low-maintenance, high-effort person who counterintuits as a matter of course, which is nice because I am looking for a job/internship/situation for the summer of '09 into the biggest economic headwind in eight decades. But, and this is important, I always walk on the sunny side of the street. Best, Erin

I felt an instant pang of fear after I read his revision written on behalf of me and my fledgling career. Was all of that really true?

In a late-night brainstorming session weeks later, we compiled a list of contacts and I drafted personalized emails for *The Colbert Report, America's Test Kitchen,* various production companies, and Fox Searchlight. Oh, and Judd Apatow. My dad forwarded my emails from his account with the subject heading "My kid, your world," knowing that his addy would get better play than ecarr@wisc.edu. After a night of pushing the refresh button on the ancient Wisconsin mail server, a forwarded response appeared in my inbox from Judd-friggen-Apatow. His response: "Is it possible that she is that cool? Happy to meet with her as long as you didn't write her email."

I called my dad and asked "How did he know?" I could sense him shrugging on the other end of the phone. *Did he write it or did I? What's the protocol here?* Dad fessed up to Judd about the edit and the cow joke being his but refused to take credit for the rest.

I was eventually connected to one of Judd's producers, Lisa, who would judge if I was as cool as the email let on. I had media classes all day, but the phone meeting was ever-present in my mind as I counted down the hours and minutes like some sort of deranged NASA clock. After trying many sitting positions in my dorm room/office as RA of the floor, I determined that standing on my lofted bed was my ultimate power position. When the California number flashed on my phone, I started the very important phone call with a cough and a loud "Hi, Lisa!"

We went back and forth, and my nervousness started to drift away. Toward the end of the call we discussed options. The internship would have to take place in Los Angeles. I knew it would be a hard sell for my situation since I had nowhere to crash. I asked if she had anything I could help out with in New York. She said no but told me that I should move to L.A. when I graduated and to get in touch then. The prospect thrilled, but I had the here and now to worry about. How could I find this kind of opportunity in New York?

I had a phone interview for *The Colbert Report* as well but am pretty sure I botched it due to inordinate fan-boying. I never heard back. Next on our list was Fox Searchlight. I knew the studio and was deeply impressed with the type of films they were putting out. Again the L.A. issue circled. The head of production emailed to say that they would be happy to consider me, and that publicity and distribution were run out of the New York office. Publicity seemed like it could be a good fit—hell, I loved talking about movies. I gchatted with Dad to prep for another nerve-racking phone call.

Me: hey dad

Dad: hey pal.

Me: i finally have that fox searchlight phone call today at 6:30

Dad: good luck with that dolly.

Me: advice = know when to talk and when not to, anything else?

Dad: go thru website and have good knowledge of what they have out and what they have coming. and the problems and opportunities of marketing those movies. who they are for and how they are positioned.

one of the things that they do very well is wait for something to catch on with a small, but important audience and then leverage that into wider awareness and interest. instead of being a studio that carpet bombs, they fight from the hills, like guerillas.

Me: oo thats good, i will surf the web today

I was well prepped, and the interview went smoothly. They said they would be in touch. I waited and waited until I finally got a phone call welcoming me as a 2009 summer intern in the publicity department. I was super jazzed. My dad responded via email with a "looks promising."

On my first day of the internship I woke up early to figure out an outfit. Jeans with a shirt and T.J.Maxx blazer seemed best. I didn't have any fancy shoes, so Converse would have to suffice. I studied myself in the mirror. My dyed-blond hair was pulled back in a way that hid my eyebrow piercing. I thought I looked fine. I figured it was okay to skip the shower and allow extra time for coffee and breakfast.

To mark the occasion, my dad said he would drive us into the city. Usually I would be relegated to the DeCamp 66, a New Jersey to Midtown express bus where talking or any sort of movement was frowned upon. Instead of sitting among strangers on a heavily air-conditioned bus, I would be able to prep for the day with my dad.

I could tell he was on edge the second we got in the car. I

asked him what his day looked like. He said, "Nope, we are going to talk about you." He told me that my outfit needed work. He then asked if I had showered. I responded defensively: "No, I showered last night. Jeez." He thought on this for a second and told me, "You are neither smart enough nor pretty enough to not shower every day."

I was taken aback. I had never given a lot of thought to how I looked before because it hadn't seemed to matter. Apparently, it mattered now. He informed me that I was about to act as his representative in New York's small media fishbowl, and the least I could do was put in a modicum of effort.

My dad lit a cigarette and blew a long stream of smoke out the window as he weaved between cars. "Let's talk about Fox Searchlight." He quizzed me on who was the president of the company. My face instantly turned red and I told him quietly I didn't know. "I know the head of my department, though," I interjected. Diana Loomis, senior vice president of Fox Searchlight Publicity: I had done a cursory Google search as per his advice. My dad launched into background on the president and what he knew about the company, before telling me he was disappointed in the substandard job I had done in preparing myself, both physically and mentally, for this job.

He went down the laundry list of things I should know to do before an interview, first day of work, or professional meeting: "Bring a notebook. Do two to three hours of research before the meeting. Arrive early. Offer to pay the check. Know their background and have questions prepared, and, above all, do your fucking homework."

My face flushed again; I felt so stupid and small. I didn't respond but instead let his reprimand sit there in the car with us. He eventually plugged in his iPod and let the music blare. The tension remained throughout the ride.

We parked the car at a garage on Eighth Avenue near his office. As we walked onto the street he put his arm around me and told me he loved me. That was the thing about his flashes of anger or disappointment: They always ended in a hug.

From the outside, the News Corp. Building on Sixth Avenue was deeply intimidating. I wondered, as I made my way through the lobby, if I had remembered to bring my ID. After checking in at the security desk I was told to take a seat. A smartly dressed woman with a blond bob came down to retrieve me. Her name was Sarah, an intern like me. Realizing I looked about five years younger than she did, I now understood my dad's concern about the lack of shower.

Sarah ran me through our duties, and I smiled pleasantly as I took in the information. It was our job to go through the five New York papers every day to see who was talking about Fox Searchlight's movies. They called each hit like this a press break. If we missed even one, it would be an embarrassing oversight for the publicity department.

After a couple of hours of reading the dailies, I was introduced to my actual supervisor, Cary, Diana Loomis's assistant. Cary wore sunglasses atop her head, four-inch heels on her feet, and had a Starbucks iced coffee, half-finished, perpetually located in her right hand. She eyed me up and down and said, "Okay, great. Sarah can show you the ropes." Clearly she had tired of the revolving door of interns. Sarah told me that she was the senior publicity intern and admitted that she was gunning for an actual J-O-B. I nodded. I told her that I just wanted to get some experience and see if publicity was for me. No threat here.

After a run to get lunch for the team (all salads), Sarah said she would introduce me around the office. It was mostly people looking up momentarily from their respective computers, but finally we knocked on a closed door and a man with a beard and warm eyes invited us in. James Finn, vice president of national publicity, invited me to take a seat, after which he asked about school and which movies of theirs I'd seen. It was comfortable and easygoing and I felt I aced the conversation. At the very end of our chat, he walked me out, smiled, and said, "Tell your dad I said hello."

That simple comment stopped me in my tracks. It made me feel like a fraud in a cheap blazer. It also made me wonder if all interns had a connection to someone of influence. Who did Sarah know? Perhaps I was naïve, thinking these opportunities were given based on merit.

The rest of the internship went a lot like that first day. Publicity didn't come naturally to me, but I arrived early and was never the first one to leave. A couple of times, I called in sick because I was nursing a hangover, but nothing that made anyone raise their eyebrows. It was clear that Cary preferred Sarah. She looked like the other women who worked there, and she knew how to anticipate their needs. And while all interns are annoying, she somehow managed to not be. I studied Sarah closely, trying out things I could mimic to be more like her, more successful. But I often found myself straddling the line between smart and clueless.

Near the end of my tenure, I was asked to take part in a publicity stunt for the movie *500 Days of Summer,* a rom-com meets dramedy starring Zooey Deschanel and Joseph Gordon-Levitt. I was tasked with handing out 250 iced coffees to hustling New Yorkers walking by Madison Square Park. Sarah took the other 250 and quickly made a head start. I plastered a grin on my face and said loudly, "Do you like coffee? Free coffee?" Most people averted their eyes and pushed past me. A couple of humans took the bait and let me prattle on about the movie (which I loved), and they told me they would check it out. Something shifted as I engaged people and talked with them about a movie I liked and cared about. It somehow became easier. If I believed in the product, it didn't feel like work.

Sarah eventually got hired for a full-time gig, and I gained experience working in the publicity department of a major studio. It turns out pushing movies is a hustle, and at the end of my tenure I knew I wanted to be a part of making movies, not selling them.

Right after I left the internship my dad forwarded this note from James Finn:

> Will hold you to that dinner. Erin is a star, and keep in touch—I'll do the same.

His kind words failed to make their intended impact. Instead I found myself once again swimming in self-doubt. Was I a star? Or was he just saying that because he was talking to my father, the *New York Times* media reporter?

When it came to my career, I now knew that David Carr's far-reaching shadow would follow me into any avenues he might open up for me. It was the price of admission for my dad helping me in this industry. His industry.

Now the question was not *if* I could get in the door, but once there, how long could I *stay*? No amount of connections or witty emails would help keep me employed in these highly sought-after jobs if I was, in fact, mediocre. I needed to find a way to be that star, to embody those words. I had survived my first internship without having made any real mark. I would have to change that.

Me: not sure where to go/what to do.

Dad: you will end up a much larger, global person. not just another brooklyn kid with a tattoo, which is great. but that kind of stuff is hard won.

Me: i am capable right?

Dad: in terms of whether you have it or not, I have a secret suspicion that you are going to end up doing SPECTACULAR things

Me: I sure hope so.

Dad: but you have to share that suspicion. However deep inside you and be willing to do whatever you have to do to make that happen. What will set you apart is not talent but will and a certain kind of humility a willingness to let the world show you things that you play back as you grow as an artist.

Talent is cheap.

Me: ok i will ponder these things. I am a carr.

Dad: that should matter quite a bit, actually not the name but the guts of what that name means.

9

Something New

"Find myself thinking about you a lot. Wondering what kind of adventures you're living, learning you are doing, tasks you are on."

At twenty-two, I was fresh out of college and stuck right at the intersection between girlhood and adulthood. Feeling wary about the trend toward the latter, I embarked on a solo move to London for my first real "job."

VICE is a media organization that originated in Canada in the early nineties as a popular counterculture magazine, covering music and parties and publishing a whole lot about drugs. There was a coolness that VICE had that tapped into the zeitgeist of youth. Looking to monetize off of this, the company started adding lieutenants to their roster who knew how to make short-form videos that could get millions of views. When I graduated from school, it was absolutely the place you wanted to work in media; still is.

My dad shot off an email to Shane Smith, one of the VICE partners, whom he had met and developed a sort of professional and personal regard for, and introduced me, and I took over the reins from there. New York was not the right spot, Shane said—too busy. No, I was going to have to cut my teeth for the company in Europe. Shane and his subordinates put forth London or Berlin. Having clumsily navigated a semester abroad in the Czech Republic with little skill in the language department, I thought that London and its English speakers made the most sense.

Now, what to pack? I took inventory of my bedroom on the second floor of our colonial house in suburban New Jersey. A collection of riot grrl zines took up space on the table next to my bed while *Buffy the Vampire Slayer* memorabilia lined the walls. The room felt dated and stale. Like it belonged to a different girl. I wouldn't be taking any of that with me. I threw in some jeans, makeup, and framed photos alongside some books, including *The Night of the Gun*.

I didn't feel excited at all as I prepared to leave for London. Instead, I felt desperate, crazy, and exhausted. I was coming off a rough summer in which alcohol had become too much of a focal point in my life. I was worried about failing in a city and country where I knew no one. On top of that I didn't have a place to live over there, and I had very little money to get by on until I figured it out. I knew I should be grateful for such an incredible opportunity, but all I could feel was anxious.

My dad took me to the airport. Part of me wondered if it was to make sure I got on the plane. I sobbed quietly as I said good-bye to him. He grabbed my arms, shook me a little, and repeated loudly, "You've got this. You've got this." He waited as I went through security. I could tell even from a distance that he had grown misty.

I didn't have a cellphone that would work abroad or a place to stay. The thought of this terrified me, but it excited something in him. I was about to go on an adventure. He sent me this email while I was in the sky flying over the Atlantic.

To: Erin Lee Carr
From: David Carr

Date: 07/30/2010
Subject: safe and sound?

Honey. we are so, so xcited for you.

please understand that you carry with you not only our love and support, but our admiration and pride in your decision to bring your ambitions roaring into the world.

your willingness to step out into the unknown and work, at a very young age, to launch an amazing professional life is congruent with who we are, but different in kind. we bring a sense of adventure to life, but often within a very small geographical footprint. you, on the other hand, are working on becoming a citizen of the world. you take our ambitions with you, our ambitions for you and for our family.

I'm sure at some point, probably sooner rather than later, you will look into the mirror and say, "what in the hell have I gotten myself into?" you did not choose the easier, softer road, but one that will ask much and give much in return. oddly enough, you will become something new by remembering who you are. You are a Carr, and that is a complicated, wondrous inheritance. That means you are tough, you are smart, you are someone others want to be around. But it also means that mistakes of hubris, excess, and indulgence will stalk you. Be vigilant to those threats, making good decisions, not every once in a while, but as a matter of course. You are a long ways from home and the consequences and rewards for your decisions will fall to you alone.

That said, please know that I am with you. I don't just want to know about the good stuff. I want to know everything. And we are not a world away, but a short flight, a quick call, a vid chat across manageable time zones.

I don't worry about you professionally. The nickel I put on you is one that you needed to get started, but I have every confidence in your industriousness, willingness and substantial skill. You are an earner, a worker among workers.

As your father, I think its okay to say that you have some work ahead of you in your personal life. The willingness to come to rest with the self, with who you are and your own company is something that you will have to master. No one else can fill the hole in Erin. Only Erin can do that. Love and be good to that person in the mirror and you will love and be good to the people around you.

It is, as they say, time to put away childish things. Or as I sometimes say, put on the big boy pants. So much can come so quickly from this and if you act as if you are in the midst of building your future, the world will unfold in wondrous ways and bury you in promises you never dreamed of. Be equal to the path you have chosen.

I can't even begin to think of all the fun you will have, the friends you will make, and the places you will go. I am deeply proud of who you are and what you are becoming. God has given you and I much—it's a long walk from the basement of my parent's home for this little family—and it makes me deeply happy that the adventure has taken this turn. Enjoy every second of it.

With love and admiration, Fahja

I arrived in England, crusty and tearful. Not the greatest start to my big, new life. I made my way via a £75 cab ride to Hampstead Heath. One of my dad's friends, in a streak of mercy, had agreed to let me crash for a couple of weeks while I navigated the housing market in London. His name was Bruce, and he was smart, funny as hell, and loved his dog Jet more than pretty much anything in the world. While we bonded over numerous pints at the local pub with Jet by our sides, I started to feel optimistic. Maybe this would work out. I could be the kid from Minnesota (by way of Jersey) that moved to London and became instantly more charming. Right?

That was always the case with me and alcohol. The booze made everything glow and my troubles fade away. But the feeling was temporary, and it usually ended with me puking all over the room I was staying in (which I actually did the first night I stayed at Bruce's—he never ratted me out).

Eventually, I found a flat in Hackney with an Italian roommate. It took 40 percent of my nebulous income, but it was safe and a twenty-minute bike ride from the VICE office.

My first day went a lot like that first day at Fox Searchlight, but with smarter fashion choices and a more expensive haircut. I stepped up my game and wore better clothes and, yes, this time I showered. People said hello, but most were too deeply engrossed in their work to pay me any mind. When I stole glances at their computer screens, I could see that they were mostly staring at iChat bubbles. At VICE, I was the only paid intern amid four of the unpaid variety, which did not enhance my popularity. The company did not make it their custom to pay interns, but a special exception was made for me after I told them I couldn't intern for free as I was not a trustfundarian (what they liked to call the young ones). They agreed to bend the rules, paying me pretty much as little as possible.

As far as the actual work went, I was given few to no tasks. The job seemed like an exercise in how quietly I could sit and not bother anyone. At night I wasn't sleeping, and during the day I wasn't being useful, and both things put me deeply on edge. Anxiety was the only thing that kept my eyes from closing in the late hours. Was I about to blow this?

Dad: this part will be the hardest in your path. you have no credentials, no portfolio, no real allies. this is where you will succeed by mettle and grit. eat some shit, bump into things, and strive, strive, strive strive. all without being annoying. tough duty.

Me: yeah thats what i have been pondering, the how to

Dad: make sure when you talk to people you seem like you are wondering and trying to figure stuff out, not whining. we both need to remember how lucky you are to be there. these are high class problems.

Me: yes i understand

Dad: am going to be home working on Trib Co. ping if you need me. and always remember to update me on your tiny victories in addition to your persistent challenges. I am so, so proud of you.

Me: 10 4. thanks fahja

Dad: tenfourxo

He was right, as always. I had to turn this job into a real job, and even though his correspondence was endowed with wisdom, he couldn't do the work for me. I had to do it myself. I look at interns now and feel a genuine pang of empathy. We are all just humans looking for something to do well that will earn us our place on this orb.

My communication with my dad during this period was frantic, intense, and voluminous. I was on the other side of the world, and yet we were so close. He wanted so badly for me to "make it," but all he could do was sit and hear about my failures and small wins after the fact.

After a couple of months, I figured out some things that I could do. I ran for coffee, organized the past archives of the magazine, took phone calls, did research, and kept my neediness to myself. I had few friends to speak of—it was hard for an American to break in socially at VICE and in London itself. Or maybe it was just me. But still, I kept at it.

I spent most weekends wandering around alone at the Tate Modern, which was fine by me. Money, or the lack thereof, was deeply problematic. Since I was really not supposed to be paid, VICE would often stiff me. My paltry paycheck was bounced around from department to department; no one wanted to pay the £1,375 per month. My math had them paying me about $480 per week, but I didn't care as long as my rent check cleared, though it usually didn't. An additional hurdle was that I did not have the proper visa to work in the country. I sent frantic emails to my dad about my pathetic attempts at trying to cover rent and food, and he electronically shook his head. Hadn't I gotten a job in order to take care of this very issue? Jill and Dad were from an earlier era, where lending money to their kid was simply not done. Having now graduated from college, I needed to figure out a way to make the money thing work on my own.

After four months, I was told that a visa was not going to come through for me to continue working at VICE. I was quietly relieved. Now, I had a reason to go home. I had given it the ol' college try, and for that I had earned a spot back in my dad's heart. The gruffness that I had felt from him during my college years began to dissipate. He had zero patience for laziness. I always knew he loved me, yes, but respect was a different matter. He needed to know that I could find a place to live, figure out money issues, and try my damnedest at a gig even when I was the lowest on the totem pole.

I would need to start the process of decision-making all over again, but at least I would be in New York, near my support network, and I wouldn't have to fear the first of the month in a way that had become unmanageable. I asked my mentor for advice on an exit strategy. Here was his reply:

> Spend a lot of time on how great it has been, and how much you have learned and then say you are probably going to split because of $ and visa. You'll know what to do.
>
> As I say, I couldn't be more impressed by you dolly.
>
> David
>
> check this . . .
>
> http://www.nytimes.com/2010/10/23/business/media/23tribune.html

And so, after all that, I was back on that airplane.

10

Holiday Party Advice

V ICE mercifully agreed to hire me to work at their New York office as an associate producer despite my unexceptional time in London. They felt bad about the visa situation and offered to give me a shot to try the gig in New York. But first I needed to secure housing that I could afford. Upon my return from London, my dad had given me a deadline: "I want you to be out of the house in two weeks." Then he explained very matter-of-factly that he did not want to start the now-normalized cycle of baby bird coming back to the nest. Tough love had worked for him, dispensed by his father, John Carr, and he wasn't about to go all soft on me. I also gleaned that I was not, let's say, the best living companion, and he needed to get me out of the house and out of his hair. I played my music loud, ate what was in the pantry without replacing it, and was basically your average shitty early-twenties adult.

My initial foray into New York living involved a spruced-up squat on Kent Avenue in Williamsburg, Brooklyn. It was the first and last apartment I interviewed for; I wasn't very picky. I knocked on the heavy metal door and heard deep footsteps shuffle toward the entrance. A tall man with a well-groomed beard and small blue eyes appeared on the other side of the door and introduced himself as Shawn. He didn't remember which candidate I was. I smiled widely and introduced myself. I knew instinctively to use the VICE name and to imply that I would be mostly at work and not one of those unfortunate roommates who spent 24/7 inside their room dicking around on Reddit.

I walked inside and took in the space; I had never seen anything like it. It was cavernous, more like a warehouse than an apartment. Salvation Army furniture littered the room. The floor was wooden and uneven but beautiful in its own right. The kitchen was covered in multicolored graffiti with a metal basket stocked with potatoes, onions, and a couple of lemons hanging down from the ceiling. This place looked lived in. Out of the corner of my eye, I saw a wooden swing hanging from the ceiling, like something you would see in Georgia outside a modest colonial with a white picket fence. I took a perch on a soft lime green couch and gave Shawn my practiced spiel, and he nodded in agreement. He laid out the downside, trying to make sure I knew what I was getting myself into. The apartment was cheap, but there was only one bathroom; would that be an issue for me? There would be five of us. Sharing one bathroom.

I weighed the pros and cons as he showed me what would potentially be my room. Small and dark with a tiny window off to the side, it had obviously been part of the original kitchen before it was subdivided. I asked about the previous roommate, a man who had in some LSD-infused trip painted a maroon man on the wall, like a prototypical caveman. I tried not to notice it. Shawn shook his head. "He partied too much and disrupted the flow of our home. Do you like to party?" He smiled slyly as he asked.

I wasn't sure what the correct answer was. I knew how I drank, but he didn't really need to know this.

"I drink every now and then," I responded nonchalantly. I

told him I would pay cash, and I had the deposit and first month all ready if he wanted to pull the trigger. I didn't even ask to meet the other roommates—that would be adding more variables to this already complicated process. I had charmed Shawn and he said yes, I could move in in a couple of weeks.

Jill and Dad agreed to spend half a day moving me and my sparse belongings into the apartment. My dad was the first to enter the space. Once again only Shawn was home. He and my dad shook hands. My dad laughed at my choice and said, "Yep, this seems about right." I elbowed him in the ribs and said, "Well, this is what I can muster on a $27,500 salary." He nodded in agreement, knowing all too well what it was like to be barely getting by. He was just glad to be rid of the visa and rent red-flare emails I continually sent him from London.

My dad dropped off the dinged-up cardboard boxes in my new hobbit hole. I was going to use the bed that the previous tenant had occupied—I had no cash for a new one. Jill was fairly disturbed, reminding me to "disinfect this entire room before sleeping in it."

We did a quick taco dinner at a restaurant nearby before they sped away back to New Jersey. I felt like I had when they'd dropped me off at college, a little nervous to begin my own life without the gimpy training wheels.

I bought some Clorox disinfectant wipes and haphazardly ran the cloth along the dusty surfaces. I needed to turn my attention toward prep for my first day at VICE New York. I spent time on the website, dutifully taking notes and trying to ascertain what material they felt allegiance toward. I fell asleep with my laptop beside me.

My alarm beeped loudly at 7 A.M. I didn't have to be at work until 10:30, but I wanted to give myself time to compose myself for the day slowly and thoughtfully. I poked my head outside of my makeshift door. The bathroom was occupied. No worries; I could do some more research on Twitter. From inside my room, I heard muffled conversations and a door opening and closing. Another person had beaten me to the morning shower. With growing annoyance, I realized that this is what life would be like with a mess of roommates. Damn, I wanted to get into the shower. My face was oddly itchy, and it was cold as hell in my room. Was the heat even on?

After waiting (not so) patiently, I finally hopped into the decrepit shower, still damp from someone else's body, and felt repulsed. Suddenly, I missed yelling loudly at my kid sister to hurry it up. I missed bouncing down the white-carpeted stairs to arrive at the dining room with my dad seated amid a flurry of newsprint. I'd ask which paper I could read, and he'd hand me the front section of *The New York Times*. The coffee pot would gurgle with anticipation, and I'd delight in the sounds of domesticity. Now, though, I was on my own.

I threw on a dress and a shitty purple peacoat I picked up from Forever 21 and rushed out the door, the wind bitterly whipping my face near the headquarters of VICE. I felt alive and full of fear. Would it be different this time?

Listening to Le Tigre, I walked briskly toward my new job. It was early December, and leaves blanketed the street. It looked idyllic. I knew this was where I was meant to be. In London, I'd felt unsure every time I stepped outside—where was I going, what tube was I taking, did I have enough money in my account to eat that day *and* pay rent for my flat at the end of the month? Here I was living cheaply and about to start a real nonintern job at my dream company. I knew how the organization was run and I was hopeful that once there, I would find my footing.

At reception, I was told to have a seat and wait for my supervisor. Glossy VICE magazines littered the textured wooden table, and I picked one up. My dad had taught me not to be that dork on her phone while waiting to meet with someone above your pay grade—it is crucial to express curiosity about the world around you instead of staring at the tiny device we use to combat our own loneliness. I registered footsteps all around me, but didn't look up until I heard my name called. A Latino man in his early thirties appeared before me. He introduced himself to me as Santiago, Santi for short. He was the director of content and my new boss. He told me there were a couple of other associate producers starting along with me; he also told me not to be nervous. Ugh, was I telegraphing my anxiety that clearly?

I was shown a small pocket of space where I would have a computer and a chair. My email was already set up from my sojourn in London, and I was notified that we had a production meeting scheduled in a couple of minutes. I walked into a small room with a large table. Six or so kids were seated there, chatting easily. I noticed a girl with voluminous brown hair looking down at her notebook. She was the only one who looked like she wasn't an extra from an American Apparel shoot. I sat next to her and she told me her name was Rhana. She pronounced it phonetically for me, "*RUN-na*. It's Palestinian," she explained.

Santiago told us in no uncertain terms that our job was to assist the producers in research for story pitches. We would act as sleuths on the Web, track interesting leads, compile the data, and deliver it in byte-sized form to a VICE producer. We were to arrive early, leave late, and not be grabby about working on our own material. Other duties included running errands, getting coffee, and the dreaded transcription of interviews. We were one step above interns, but barely.

I took a seat at my new desk as a manic goatee-sporting man ran over to me. His name was Brian, and he explained to me that I would be wrangling post details for the MTV show *The*

Vice Guide to Everything. I needed to track down releases and make sure the production bibles—black binders filled to the brim with daily call sheets, music cue sheets, and personal and location releases (the sexy stuff)—were complete and ready to go. I made a mental note that it seemed like you needed to be very organized to make television, or find someone else to organize it for you. When I asked Brian a follow-up query, I couldn't help but focus on the gumball machine on the corner of his desk. Rather than gum or M&M's, the machine was filled with aspirin. Which he proudly took like vitamin C tablets for hangovers and/or deep, unrelenting migraines due to stress. The message was clear: Here, pain, often brought on by excessive drinking and partying, was to be worn like a badge of honor. I would be expected to keep up.

I had been working in the New York office for just two weeks when VICE threw their annual holiday party. I arrived at the office nervous as hell. It seemed like one of the requirements of having a job there was being blessed in the looks department. While I do not necessarily resemble a ferret, my looks are not generally something people remark upon when meeting me. I felt insecure and desperately ugly in the unisex bathroom as I changed into a purple sequined dress that I got in London. I was convinced it could transform me into a full-figured Bond girl instead of the less than stellar woman I saw in the mirror. I added a giant fake-fur coat to complete the ensemble. But perhaps the kicker was that my face was covered in Band-Aids. I had developed impetigo from living in the squat. My dad had wisely cautioned me to sit this one out based on my condition, but I refused.

On the neon-lit party bus, I settled in next to the ad dudes and took giant slugs from a bottle of Jim Beam. The bus reminded me vividly of being the odd kid at summer camp with no partner to talk to. I prayed the booze would work quickly and, sure enough, there came the warm blanket coating my tongue and making everything feel just a tad brighter. I closed my eyes and reminded myself to monitor my intake—this was my first Christmas party at my first real job. I needed to get in and out of this without undergoing a colossal embarrassment.

The potion worked its magic. I strolled into that glittering Russian bazaar like I owned the place. I spotted Rhana, and she took in my appearance: "It looks like you're already having fun," she remarked. I raised my eyebrows at the drink that had somehow appeared in my hand. I confessed to her that I thought she was smart and cool and I wanted to be *very* close work allies. She responded nicely, but I could tell she was waiting to see what happened next. I got out on the dance floor and busted a move. *This is all going to work out!* my brain shouted. And that is the last thing I remember clearly.

I woke up the next day in my loft bedroom, in someone else's old bed, forgetting for a second where I was. I still had the dress on, the sequins pinching my skin and the giant fur coat draped over me like a blanket. At least no one was in bed with me. I tried to cobble together fragments of memory. Did I really go up to the head of the company and strike up a slurred conversation? Did I try to hit on that older ad exec? What else? I had just started this gig, and I knew my behavior wouldn't fly. I checked the time—*fuck*, I had to shower and get to the office.

I skulked in barely on time and lowered myself into my desk chair, concentrating solely on not puking up the bread and whiskey in my stomach. A PR guy spotted me and said, "Carr: Top Five Drunkest." He repeated it three times. I could only assume he was saying that out of the hundreds of employees, I had made quite the impression. My face was a deep scarlet by the time he walked away. I had been found out. The drink, shame, hangover cycle was alive and well in me. The impetigo would go away in a couple of weeks, but my reputation would require a more dedicated recovery.

I didn't tell my dad about the holiday party. I just couldn't; I needed this job to work. We'd shared almost everything about our lives up until that point, including alcohol-related lapses in judgment, but this felt different because I knew it would keep happening if I continued to drink. I also couldn't bear hearing him say "I told you so." I always thought that when I entered the real world I would put away childish things, so to speak, and for me that meant my drinking. I worried that this was not the case, that I couldn't stop. So I did what a lot of people do when it comes to drinking mistakes: I pushed the feelings deep inside of me and ignored them.

11

Far from the Tree

Growing up, in the years before high school, alcohol was not something I thought about too much. My stepmom would have an occasional glass of red wine, but I never saw my dad drink or talk about missing it. My father did not drink alcohol—it was just a fact—like he worked at *The New York Times* and enjoyed popcorn with extra butter at the movies. I once saw a case of O'Doul's on his work bench in our basement, and when I asked about it he told me to look at the label. I peered closer. "Oh, it is nonalcoholic beer." He nodded and told me out of the corner of his mouth that it "didn't taste the same but it was better than nothing."

It turned out that alcoholism and ongoing struggles with booze were some of the many traits I shared with my father. My dad knew intimately the siren call of substances and the temporary relief they offered. He had empirical evidence that his genetic code, when combined with vodka, led to handcuffs and treatment centers. Still, long-term sobriety eluded him for decades. Our birth changed all that. After Meagan and I were born he remained fully sober for fourteen years. Until something changed. And he began to drink again, on and off.

. . .

When I was seventeen, in the summer of 2005, Dad was supposed to take my sisters and me up to the family cabin in the Adirondacks. Jill was on a work trip. I was obsessed with television at the time (still am), and I secretly delighted as the hours dragged on and it started getting late, as it meant we might not go to the cabin after all. My sisters, however, were a different story. "Aren't we supposed to be going soon?" Meagan asked as we heard our dad shuffling around on the porch. "Shh," I said. "*Buffy* is on. Let's talk after this episode." She went back upstairs with a huff.

After he called the three of us to come outside and head out, I found my dad moving quietly around in the dark, leafing through papers on his makeshift desk. He was breathing heavily. I asked if he was okay. He turned to me, and his eyes were bloodshot. I had never seen him like this. He muttered a semblance of a response that indicated I was not to ask any more questions. I felt silenced and uncomfortable. He was the one making us late.

"I'm hungry," I told him.

"We'll eat on the road," he barked back.

As we started our drive away from our home in Montclair, the yellow lines began to swerve underneath us. We looked at one another, totally unsure of what to do. Meagan was the first to speak. "What is going on, Dad? You don't seem all right. You need to pull over." He sighed loudly, turned on his blinker, and moved the wheels to the right, hitting the gas pedal. There was a loud blaring honk as a big SUV missed us by inches. The horn felt like it lasted for minutes.

"What is wrong with you?" I yelled as he turned off at a gas station. My baby sister and twin were fearful and quiet. Meagan got out of the car and dialed a family friend who told us to call a cab. Dad insisted we get back in the car, and we drove the eight minutes back to our darkened house in New Jersey. He had been drinking. He could have killed us and himself that night. He drank more when he got home. We called Jill and told her what had happened. She was horrified but not surprised. He had been off the wagon for months.

There would be a few more nights like that one in his life, a few more relapses before he got clean again, but nothing that quite matched the level of terror for me of that first one. Months later he was pulled over driving to my high school for a college informational seminar for parents on finding the right school and paying for it. He never made it to the seminar. The cops arrested him en route and my dad was forced to forfeit his license for more than a year. Who drives their kids drunk? Who drinks on the way to a parent-teacher conference? I learned quickly that the circumstances did not matter when it came to my dad and alcohol. He was powerless.

He called one morning, and I knew something was wrong the second I heard him at the other end of the line. I was in year two at VICE and just trying not to drown. His voice was raspier than usual, and his speech was careful and deliberate. It sounded like he was on the street when he should have been in his cube at the *Times*. He asked if I had time to meet in Williamsburg later that evening. I said of course, without hesitation. The call ended abruptly and without him telling me he loved me, which was odd. I had to sit at work for the next six hours wondering what on earth he was going to tell me.

I met my dad at El Moderno, a bar in Williamsburg off the Lorimer Street stop of the Brooklyn-bound L train. I rushed there, a knot of fear resting in my stomach as I walked the fifteen minutes from my desk to the bar. He was already there when I arrived. What greeted me looked like my dad, and yet it didn't. He was seated in a booth, his eyes unfocused and glassy as he squinted at his BlackBerry. Next to him sat an empty martini glass, still frosted from the chilled vodka. I approached the table. He looked embarrassed but stood up and pulled me into a bear hug, both of us holding on a little too long. His eyes remained downcast until I threw my messenger bag on my side of the red leather booth.

"So, this is starting again," I muttered, unsure if I should go with humor or seriousness when approaching my dad's relapse. It had been years since the last time. We thought he had experimented back then, and once recovered, it was over. That is how the recovery narrative goes. Alcoholic gets and stays clean. Your brain and body know what is forbidden territory.

"You know, I am not quite sure how I got here," he mused, almost as if I wasn't there. As if he were talking to someone else. "But I have some guesses." A cute waitress sauntered over to our table and asked if he wanted another round. He ordered a martini. I ordered a glass of pinot grigio. This would be the first drink we ever had together. It felt nothing like a celebration. Not even close.

I could sense that he was at least a couple of drinks deep when we started to talk and that slur came back. I knew it because I had heard my own voice fall into it on occasion.

"Where in the relapse are we? Did this just start?"

He shook his head. To lighten the mood, I started to tease him about the shirt he was wearing. It was an oversized blue shirt with a sort of gingerbread man on it. It seemed a bit childlike, not at all his typical uniform. He stared at me and said, "Don't you say that. My sweeto gave this to me." We were back to silence. The wine didn't help me much; I would need a couple more glasses before I felt any sort of effect.

Finally, I asked the only real question that mattered: "Why are you drinking and do you want to stop?"

"I do want to stop, I know I *need* to stop." He described to me what life had been like lately: Twitter, covering the glittering parties, the deadlines that followed. He continued, "It's just all the stuff at work, the parties, the people. I just felt like I wanted to be part of it for once." He looked down. He knew how he sounded. He added, "It's hard to come into middle age. It doesn't feel like I should be here yet, but I look in the mirror and this is what I am left with."

His mind was quick as ever, but his body and his health made it clear that he needed to slow down. As a deeply ambitious person, he resented it. I was unsure how to respond. It wasn't something I had ever really thought about. For the first time, my dad was revealing himself to me to be a flawed human being, not just my father. Not just the writer. But even then I understood that middle age had not led to the relapse; he himself had. That was what I needed to focus on.

"What will happen if you continue drinking?" I wondered out loud. "It'll just get worse, I imagine. We've watched this episode before." I reminded him of the detox that followed his drunk-driving arrest a few years back, the rebuilding of family trust. The necrotizing pancreatitis that left him with diabetes. I knew that alcohol and diabetes could be a lethal combination, and yet here we were.

He seemed genuinely mystified but knew it had to be a short run. His forehead wrinkled as he joked about being one of the incurable ones. We both ordered another drink. I knew it was bad form to drink with your relapsed parent, but I was going to *need* a drink if I was going to get through what came next.

He told me Jill was upset with him; I knew how she felt. I felt resentful seeing him repeat the same behavior, for putting his health in jeopardy right in front of my eyes. But I didn't have it in me to reprimand him. Instead I held my anger deep within. I was twenty-three years old and didn't have the faintest idea about what advice to offer my dad. He didn't care; our relationship knew very little in the way of boundaries. I could yell at him, but what good would it do? He already hated himself.

Then he said something that made me panic. "I was standing on the platform, trying to get here on the L train. I thought, just for a second, about throwing myself down into the subway and just letting it fucking hit me." He stared at me. I asked if this was a joke, and he noncommittally shrugged. I had never heard him admit a suicidal thought before. He was hurting. We needed to get him into treatment. Again.

I felt a mixture of emotions as we made our way through our drinks. I felt a responsibility to let him know that I loved him unconditionally. I also knew, from previous experiences, that there needed to be consequences for addicts that did not change. I felt stuck and unsure what to do or say.

And then it was over. After my second drink and I am guessing his fourth, he called it a night. I hailed him a cab, feeling frantic about the idea of him on a subway platform. I asked if he could go to a meeting tomorrow or a detox. He assured me he would figure it out and would be on his way back to sobriety, back to being my dad. He held me close as we said goodbye and thanked me for loving him no matter what. I started to cry and he said, "None of that, now. You are a Carr. You are strong." A tear leaked down his face as he said this. He finally climbed into the car and told the driver to head toward Midtown. I slammed the yellow door closed and looked at him through the window, for a second wanting to get in and make sure he got home okay.

I smiled weakly and he waved. The cab pulled away and I stood there for a moment taking it in, sobbing.

I sped toward my local wine store and grabbed a big bottle of cheap white wine. Tears lined my face and the cashier made no attempt at small talk. I took it back to my apartment and said nothing to my roommates, drinking it glass by glass until I was numb and pretty much blackout drunk. I thought about emailing him, but I had nothing to say. I was too far gone.

12

The House of Many Felled Trees

**"Austin was kind of a revelation, you need
to move here and then I need to follow."**

My dad loved Twitter. With twenty-nine thousand tweets
and a follower base of more than four hundred thousand,
his feed was the perfect mixture of high- and lowbrow content.
People followed in droves to read his honest, funny, and human
interpretation of the world around him in 140 characters or less.
I was one of those 400K, and as a blood relative I got a follow
back. I was one of the few.

After his death, a sexbot hacked the account and started
posting highly disturbing content on his page, so *The New York
Times* handed the reins over to me. I downloaded the archive
and began sifting through the deluge of information. I tapped a
friend to create a data set for my dad's Twitter account. I sent
her the feed, but felt strange doing so. What was I trying to find,
and was it my information to even give away?

I was unsurprised when she handed me his most hashtagged
phrases: #SXSW was number one. South by Southwest is an annual music and film festival in Austin, Texas. The carnitas tacos
are deluxe and so is the town. Janet Pierson runs the epic film
portion of the festival and she and my dad became fast friends
when he started going in 2009. It was one of his absolute favor-

ite events to attend. He told me resolutely that I would feel the same.

I was in the middle of my second year at VICE in 2012 when I raised my hand during a meeting with my techie overlords. "SXSW is coming up, and I think I should go and interview for a series of roundups with the smartest people in town." I stammered when I spoke, still unsure of my place within the larger system. "I think we can share our brand and get video with people we wouldn't normally have access to." It was a fine idea, but in reality I just wanted to go to SXSW to meet up with my dad. The bearded guy with glasses typed it into his computer and said he would think about it. I set about stalking the forums to see who would be attending that might be open to being interviewed. I needed a way to justify the trip.

My boss bought my story, and in a few short months I, along with my co-worker Sean, was boarding a plane to Dallas where we would pick up a rental car and drive to Austin. All the direct flights were long gone, but I didn't mind as I was on a *paid* work trip. I felt like this was the start of something great. I emailed my dad and updated him on my arrival status. He responded in minutes.

Hoped u packed warm hoss. In the badge line, which is epic.

The badge he was talking about was a golden ticket to all things festival related. I had gotten press credentials and the thousand-dollar entry fee waived, and this was my key to the festivities.

We arrived at our Airbnb. Some smart Austinite had rented out their one-bedroom apartment, where we would switch off between the bed and the couch for four hundred bucks a night. After dropping off our stuff, we walked toward downtown, the hot, dense air sticking to us. There was an energy in the air, music wafting in waves from streets we had yet to walk. I was filled with a sense of hope and possibility—I could do the things I dreamed about all those years ago in my pop-culture-covered bedroom in northern New Jersey.

The next day I, along with a few dozen others, received an email invitation from my dad.

From: David Carr
To: David Carr
Bcc: Erin Lee Carr
Date: 03/10/2012
Subject: An invite from Jenna, Brian and David
at the House of Many Felled Trees

To all the talk about SxSW being a goat rodeo that has jumped the shark on the way to nuking the fridge, we'd like to say: Not so fast. We are part of the crowd, the ones that love it here. Especially when we end up eating food from a truck and drinking beer from a tub, as we will on Sunday night at 6pm, outside our room at Hotel San Jose on South Congress. Management here has apparently caught on and Carr is upstairs in room 54 this year, so no big mud patio and a much smaller gathering on two balconies. Please RSVP if you are coming and don't pass along or post about it. We'll be done by 8.

The secret invite to his party. He was known for throwing raucous parties with bathtubs full of beer that he did not drink. It had now been a year since his most recent relapse. He would crank up Beck's album *Guero* and showcase his ridiculous Midwestern moves on the dance floor. He did not care who was watching, and it showed. One might guess that this would be embarrassing for his mid-twenties daughter. One would guess wrong. Frankly, I was impressed. It was one of the many things

I learned from how he chose to live his life—be your own damn thing.

I wandered into the San Jose in my lace shirt-skirt combo, very New York and off-scene. I took in the party while I cracked a bathtub beer. My dad was hosting with known wunderkind Brian Stelter and the effortlessly cool Jenna Wortham. All three worked at the *Times* and were mingling comfortably with the tech glitterati. I went in for the hug with my dad, and he started introducing me as his kid who worked for VICE. People were kind, but I could tell instantly that I was not who they really wanted to be speaking with at such an event. I returned to the bathroom to retrieve another beer from the tub, and before I knew it I was seven beers deep. I didn't like to drink around my dad, but I couldn't really stop myself. I didn't like being watched by someone who understood what that need felt like for me: less normal and more of an impulse I couldn't ignore. I found myself getting louder, funnier, even joining in on the dance party.

When the shindig grew too loud, my dad decided it was time to move the crew to the Bravo tent. He drove us there, sober as a nun, laughing the whole way. I marveled at his ease in navigating conversations, relationships, different age groups. Even with early twentysomethings, he never looked uncomfortable. He wanted to be where the action was, and the action wanted him. In the flashy tent, I guzzled the blue shots being passed around. I went to the bathroom and put my head between my legs and took a deep breath. I felt fuzzy and knew I was nearing the line between consciousness and a blackout. My body said stop, but my brain said drink a little more.

Next on our bar crawl was a dance party for Foursquare. With the exception of my dad, everyone was buzzed at this point. I wondered if it was starting to get boring for him. Stories were repeated ad nauseam. The dance music drowned that out so we busted a move.

In the wee hours of the morning, my dad decided to call it a night and suggested I do the same. If he was concerned about my drinking, he didn't say so. I was one of many kids having a wild time at the festival. I had interviews to conduct the next day. I obliged but only because there was no more free gin. I made my way out to the front of the club, waved over a rickshaw, and gave the sturdy-looking driver my Airbnb address. The sky started to spit out water, coating me in a small mist. I searched my purse for my phone and took my badge off to put in said purse. The rickshaw hit a bump and my drunken hands lost their grip on the thousand-dollar badge. I watched as it sailed out onto the street behind me. I knew I should say something to my driver, but my drunken stupor rendered me silent. I faced forward and felt the rain on my face. Blackouts have a way of creating apathy.

The next morning I woke up and realized first thing that my badge was missing. I immediately headed back to the expo cen-

Dancing like everyone's watching at SXSW.

ter where I spotted the sign: WE ARE NOT RESPONSIBLE FOR LOST OR STOLEN BADGES. Curious how I missed that the day before. I wondered if my Irish charm could convince the lady in the booth to take pity on me. I steeled myself as I walked up to the woman, who in slow-motion shook her head. I continued to plead my case, to no avail. I was the idiot that lost her badge on the first night of the festival.

I had interviews set up back at the Airbnb so I raced back, golden-ticket-less. I attempted to get through a sit-down with Iranian activist and journalist Saman Arbabi, but I felt waves of nausea grip me as I asked him about the Internet and how it related to promoting dissent. My vision blurred and my stomach began to churn. I excused myself and vomited in the bathroom as quietly as possible, running the faucet to drown out the sound. I returned to our makeshift set and kept my eyes cast down until I started asking questions again. Was the camera even rolling? I felt like I was going to pass out.

I made it through the interview, but as soon as I closed the door behind my guest, someone I had been thrilled to speak to, I reviewed the interview tape. It was unusable. My questions were incoherent and the back-and-forth was a mess.

Waves of self-hatred began to wash over me. Why was everyone else able to drink and do their jobs? I was mystified and miserable about my inability to stop drinking past a certain point. My lack of control around alcohol was affecting my work life. It was undeniable at this point.

When I got back to New York my dad asked how the rest of the trip went. I cannot remember his tone, though I wonder now if it was a leading question that I was not ready to answer. I told him it was a smashing success. I couldn't bear to share the truth. With him, or with myself.

13

Stories Are There for the Telling

"When it is scary outside and people are fearing for their
futures, they like to gather in a dark room and stare at
a screen, holding hands against the gloom."

My dad knew how to tell a story, in all formats. Whether it was a bedtime story he told us girls, his husky voice in an NPR interview with Terry Gross, or in a written column eviscerating the *Chicago Tribune*'s new management, he knew instinctively how a story should come together. I could hear his voice clearly through each medium. I yearned to know these secrets, too.

We began a more official spate of mentoring during my time at VICE in New York. When I started there, I was super green, but I knew I didn't want to just assist people mindlessly for the next five years, a role young women were often relegated to. My father knew that one of the key ingredients to success was repetition and familiarity. In the beginning he instructed me to watch all that I could and get a feel for what "hit" and what fell flat. My dad's media consumption was massive, and he expected those around him to keep up. I would get countless emails about watching a new show on IFC or a viral video on YouTube or an important feature doc that had just been at Sundance. When I expressed derision or criticism, he would remark, "You aren't watching to be a hater. Please turn off that side of your brain and just listen. There are many things for you to learn."

When we discussed media, which was often, he'd give me his version of homework. These lessons often took place on the back porch of his house—his workroom, where he could be found smoking and wearing the headset that he would take off every so often and toss on the green metallic table with a clank. The family dog, Charlie, sat at his feet, not even bothering to get up when I would come into the makeshift office. She knew who to get up for. My dad would type away, all the while issuing commands from the corner of his mouth.

At one session he attempted to help me focus on which stories were worth covering, and through whose lens: "Okay, so we talked about what you are liking. Can you make a list of people whose careers you admire—four should work. Use the Google machine and trace back how and when they started their careers. Can you do that and report back?" He looked away from the keyboard and up at me to study my response. I eyed the cigarettes on the table and just for a second wanted one.

Instead I answered his question: "Yeah, I can do that. Might take a little while."

He responded, "Well, you aren't home for a while and I'm busy. Can we talk tomorrow, maybe late?"

I nodded my head, and he reverted his attention back to the glowing screen in front of him. I'd been dismissed.

I went back up to my old bedroom and checked Twitter. I wasn't even sure what I wanted to be, let alone who I wanted to be. I opened up Word and saw the cursed cursor blinking at me. *Let's start simple,* I thought. What did I love? I'd had a sort of religious experience when I watched *Enron: The Smartest Guys in the Room,* a documentary detailing the vast corruption and shocking demise of the energy-trading Enron Corporation. It was a dark, acerbic investigation by filmmaker Alex Gibney.

Best of all, the film was a living document that showed those scoundrels for who they really were. I would love to work on something like that.

Then there was Liz Garbus's HBO documentary film *There's Something Wrong with Aunt Diane,* an investigation into a car accident that was less about the crime and more about what it means to be a mother in the twenty-first century. Her film haunted me. I added her name to the Word doc. I had watched *Capturing the Friedmans* about seventeen times, so I thought *Maybe Andrew Jarecki?* I didn't know who to choose as my fourth, but I knew I wanted it to be a woman. I spent hours trying to figure out the next name before it hit me. I had recently met a young woman named Lena Dunham at my dad's request, and she had the firepower that I thought could translate. She made the list. So now I had four, and three out of four of them were documentary filmmakers that had made dark, disquieting films. I had an answer, but it didn't seem like a financial possibility. I turned in my assignment and waited for a response.

A couple of days later, he called me. "Good work," he said. "Let's see how we can get in contact with these people. First up, meet Lena and Alex in person, if they have time to spare."

I wanted to stay at VICE but I also wanted to figure out possible next steps. It had been drilled into me early on that if you like the work you do, then it doesn't feel like work. Could I be a documentary filmmaker? This exercise helped me realize that I had to figure out what made my heart beat faster. I needed to recognize the topics that I clicked on time and time again to find out more, just like these filmmakers had done. I could start by making short films about ideas and problems I was obsessed with and go from there. I loved mysteries and crime, but that seemed too vague. After being assigned to VICE's science and technology website Motherboard, I realized I was completely obsessed with the Internet and the huge range of stories it created. I mostly gravitated toward crime, sex, and weapons, but all had to have a twenty-first-century slant to make them newsy and interesting to a media-saturated audience.

At Motherboard, I assisted on a variety of projects until I felt it was time to start pitching my own ideas. But how to find the right story to pitch? With the help of my secret weapon, my dad, I was able to focus-group and separate the good ideas from the bad. Even then, I realized that this was an incredibly privileged perch from which to launch my early career. I vowed to take advantage of it but also to do the same for others, if and when it came to be my turn.

My dad told me time and time again to question what audiences are curious about. What drives media consumers? Why is anyone going to sit down and watch this video? In response, we developed the "cultural nerve" strategy. This meant that when considering whether to produce a video, a central question had to be asked: What is it about the story that touches on a cultural nerve? This hypothesis was never more proven than with a short film I produced called *Click, Print, Gun*.

Faith Gaskins, a field producer with VICE's HBO team, kept seeing a name pop up in her newsfeed: Cody Wilson. He was a twentysomething anarchist who vehemently believed that it was his right to open-source and manufacture 3D-printed firearms. Faith pitched Cody for a segment for the VICE HBO show, and while I believe it was mulled over for a couple of weeks, the powers that be ultimately passed. She handed what we call a one-pager over to me, with the message "Maybe this would be a good story for you?"

Faith is an unfailingly generous person. She could have kept that information to herself, locked away in some folder on her dusty laptop, but instead she chose to help out a fellow producer to see if the idea could work for someone else. Every day I try and remind myself of this lesson.

I knew the story could go viral the second I got that one-pager. I reached out to Cody by email.

He responded a few hours later.

Erin,

I'd be happy to participate. Perhaps there are some project updates in which you'd be interested.

crw

Before I knew it, I was on a plane to Austin to meet the man on the other end of the email.

When I stepped off the plane and into the hot, dense Texas air, I was relieved when I saw I'd received no word from Cody trying to pull out of the interview. My cameraman, Chris, picked me up in a rental car, honking the horn as he waved excitedly.

We arrived at the slightly abandoned-looking warehouse that was Cody's work space, and I called him. No answer. I shot him a text as I leaned against the hot car, trying to clear my head and not overthink it. Eventually Cody strode out with a grin on his face and reached his hand out to shake mine. I grinned back and introduced myself. He eyed me up and down.

Over the course of the next couple of days, Cody introduced us to his friends and business associates but mainly stuck to his ideas and philosophy. I felt the nervousness drain away as we struck up a rhythm. I was like a kid in summer, plotting capers and building forts. He had a way of making eye contact that made you feel like no one else was in the room. (Don't worry—this is not a story about how we fell in love. One of the many salient things my dad taught me is don't fuck your subjects.)

During our filming, Cody 3D-printed the lower receiver for an AR-15 semiautomatic firearm. The print could take up to a day, so we were sure to get backups from allies of his. His ideology ran the gamut, but what he valued most was freedom. He explained over beers that he loved America and was a patriot but wanted the technological expansion that had been in the works for decades to continue, untouched by the government. He would fight (using words) for that right and was just fine with being the poster child for the wiki weapons movement. In fact, he enjoyed his bad-boy image, as it set him apart from his conventional contemporaries.

I felt conflicted. I believed in freedom, but as a bleeding-heart liberal I despised guns. They extinguish life, and I would be glad to see them removed from our planet. That said, I did shamelessly go out into the backwoods and fire some guns with this gang of motley boys. I will hand in my liberal/Planned Parenthood ID next time I hit up the DMV.

The 3D-printed gun worked. Back at the hotel I watched the footage late into the night, making sure the story was there. The trip had been a success, despite some nerves early on.

When I got back to New York the next day I walked through the VICE offices with purpose. I had the footage on me and headed straight toward postproduction. Chris, the editor I had been working with for about a year, was seated in his office, enjoying a cup of coffee when I entered. I told him about the scenes I had put together during filming—a tour of Cody's room, showing us the CAD file, his arsenal, the bullets and the trip to the woods to see if the gun actually worked. Chris looked surprised; he had requested more B-roll on shoots, and I had delivered. He was one of many mentors whose words were gospel to me.

As the edit commenced, Chris mentioned that the film lacked context—yes, the material with Cody was eye-popping, but without another voice it felt one-sided, almost like we agreed with his point of view. I told my dad about it over the phone.

"Well, where did you hear about the story?"

"I heard about it through Faith."

"Yes, but where did she find out about the story?"

I instant-messaged her, and she said she saw a great version of it in *The New York Times*.

"Yep, here we come full circle. She saw it in the *Times*."

He laughed quietly and said, "Yes, I thought as much. My buddy Nick Bilton wrote it. Email him to see if he can work you in. Gotta jet, on deadline."

I heard a click before I even had a chance to respond.

I've learned since then that you do not take credit for an idea that does not belong to you. Including Nick in the narrative of the story gave voice to the legitimate ethical questions that we as the filmmakers wanted to ask. Nick agreed to sit for an interview while I was shooting another project in L.A. He appeared just on time, answered questions succinctly, and asked if we were close to being done around the one-hour mark. The interview was crucial for the short film.

I begged VICE to host a press screening for the Web film, and they obliged without hesitation. We did it at the Soho House, a trendy private Manhattan club with a screening room. I invited filmmaker Alex Gibney, who did me the honor of attending. My dad was one of the first to arrive and strolled up to me with a look of intent. He wrapped me up into his arms and told me how proud he was. The hug lingered.

He prayed, wished, and ultimately knew that his kids would be successful. Not just because we were his, but because we, as preemies, thrived early on in a world that did not necessarily want us. Maybe it made the sacrifice worth it? I wasn't always so sure, but that night in that glittering city, a night that I had worked so hard to get to, I believed in our story, in the success of it.

14

Tyranny of Self

Dad: i am looking for something i want you to read. hold on a sec. here it is:

https://www.wsj.com/articles/SB122178211966454607

Me: got it.

Dad: david foster wallace giving commencement at kenyon. he killed himself, but his writing on the tyranny of self, something you and i both deal with, is awe inspiring.

Me: that is true.

Dad: i should work on mowing the lawn you know that I adore you and thinking of the world of you. there is a freshness and rigor in your voice. an awareness of things beyond you that i find really exciting. i know there is probly plenty of mayhem out of view but i just feel really good about who you are becoming. as papa would say "i think you are neat."

Tyranny of self was one way to put it. Extreme ambition could be another way to describe it.

How was my dad able to figure so much out in such a short life? Many have asked me this question. I thought a lot about it and have come up with a series of answers:

1. He was naturally brilliant.
2. His work ethic far outmatched most civilians'.
3. There was a certain degree of mania and/or narcissism involved in his personality that drove him to extremes.

My brain immediately creates an excuse as soon as I type this. I know that most successful people are, to a degree, selfish and careerist. You need to put yourself first in order to get to that next level. I, too, have inherited this gene, and would rather spend time trapped in my apartment making movies than listening to a friend drone on about that crazy dream they had last night.

My dad could be ruthless, cutting, and focused solely on himself. His program of recovery curbed these selfish impulses, but he and I knew they were permanently there. He was good at hiding them as needed. He always made the joke that he was constantly trying to figure out the right way to be a human being. Almost as if it were a character he was trying out. As a sober person, he lost the ability to cut loose through alcohol and cocaine, so he tried to find other ways. For some time, I was convinced that his Twitter feed was more important than whatever I had to say. Too much coffee or expensive food, micro Internet celebrity and the attention it garnered, smoking insane amounts of cigarettes, driving very fast. These were all ways he could still be "bad."

Driving was a particularly hazardous endeavor with him. Due to a Hodgkin's lymphoma diagnosis at thirty-five, he endured radiation, which corroded the muscles in his neck, and thus he had a hard time looking fully left or right. Instead of fixing the problem or asking me to check his blind spot, he would swing our Explorer into the lane he wanted to be in, sometimes putting on his blinker, but mostly not. He just assumed that a car would move out of the way for him. This was true on the highway and in life.

In the summer of 2014, we were alone at our cabin in the Adirondacks. Something had happened with his column days earlier, and he was in an irritable mood. We got dinner at the local chicken shack, a beloved place called Hattie's. I ordered the same thing that he did. Big-boy order of fried chicken with a side of collard greens and mashed potatoes with a generous amount of gravy piled on top. Diet Coke accompanied the order, naturally. Our stomachs and hearts full, we piled back into the car. He clicked through his music until he found the Replacements, a band that he adored. It was dark now. He cranked the music up almost as loud as it could go. The car began to shake from the bass. It was too loud for me. I watched as he raced back to our green cabin, pushing eighty miles an hour on mountain highways that were known to hide deer. I shouted at him, "Maybe we should slow down!" He grunted in response, paying me no mind. I started to sweat and had a sick thought: *This is how I die, in this car with my dad.* My heart raced as I watched him, window open, cigarette smoking, foot on the gas. Extreme in so many ways. He did not fear death as others might; instead, I imagine he courted it, taunted it, as if to say, "Look at what I've been through already, and I'm still here."

We arrived back home safely, against the odds, and I slammed the door. "That was way too fast. It wasn't safe." He reminded me through gritted teeth to never tell him how to run his show. With that he walked into the cabin living room and closed the door. I retreated to my side of the house and thought about what had just happened. Was I overreacting? I didn't feel like a cautious person. Why couldn't my dad hear me when I told him I wasn't feeling safe? It was like he was willing to do anything to protect me, except when it intersected with his control issues.

When it came to that territory, he was unwilling to compromise. Or was there something about me that made him push the mental IGNORE button?

I stayed mad at him for days. The next morning, I glowered at him as he made coffee for the both of us. He just could not stand anyone telling him what to do. I wondered what he was like at work, with bosses and deadlines. Navigating the internal political waters at the *Times* surely required making compromises.

Even though I was distraught, I didn't bother calling my sisters to intervene on my behalf. I had the distinct impression that nothing I or my sisters said would elicit meaningful change; only he had the power to dictate that.

As the days passed I tried to just forget about the incident and move past it, but when he asked me if I wanted to get dinner, saying he was tired of hot dogs on the family stove, I shook my head. I lied and told him I wasn't feeling well. I didn't want to get in the car with him again. I didn't like not having a way out. He likely didn't care.

15

Choose Wisely

It all started with some oversharing. When I set out to write this book, I posted on Facebook: "Hive-mind: Have any of you guys done writing residencies? Do you have a creative place that you loved when you made your doc/book/project? I would love your feedback . . . xo." Helpful suggestions trickled in, and then I saw that my ex-boyfriend Paul had posted a comment on my status. I clicked on the notification and saw the words "locked in my bedroom crying." I instinctively smiled, flushed with a mixture of excitement and dread. He knew what I was going to write about and asked to meet with me.

I agreed to meet Paul for coffee in Park Slope, Brooklyn. Originally he suggested dinner, but that sounded too intimate and time-consuming for this confrontation.

I was already seated when he walked in. I had to admit, he looked good. We started with some small talk, but he was determined to cut to the chase, questioning me about my book. As I told him about my writing, he interjected with "But are you going to talk about that one night?"

I said yes, then tried to lessen his fears by saying I would like to interview him and get his side of the story. I knew I was by no means an angel in my version.

"I just . . . I don't know why you need to go into that whole thing. Everyone will know it's me."

"Who, our four mutual friends?" I replied.

He looked down. "Everyone, everyone who knows you is going to read it and know it's me. I have never acted like that since then and I would prefer if that is not what I am known for."

I nod.

"Do I have any rights here?" he said.

I could not help but feel sad for him. "Well, I can't print libel or lies. It has to be what happened."

He looked down again. "That's what I am worried about."

A few minutes later we got up to leave. I almost tripped on the way out. When I got dressed that morning I had chosen heels for this very moment, imagining a graceful exit as I walked away from the table with Aretha Franklin pounding in my head. But instead, we shuffled out the door together. It wasn't triumphant or empowering. It was more depressing and uncomfortable.

As we stood on the sidewalk I asked in a hopeful tone, "Do you feel better now that we've talked?"

"No, I actually feel worse."

I walked him to the subway off of the Seventh Avenue stop. The stop that we used when we lived together.

"Do you remember the last time you spoke to my dad?"

"Actually I do. He literally threatened my life and then told me he loved me." He laughed. "It was the strangest, craziest phone call I had ever gotten, but it ended with 'I love you.'" He shook his head.

"He loved you because I loved you."

Until I didn't.

According to my family, when it came to romance, I have always picked "eight balls," those who are just this side of crazy—possessing some sort of mental or alcohol disorder, but most likely easy on the eyes. In twelve-step programs, they refer to this as your "picker" being broken. You pick the wrong partner because your brain automatically gravitates toward dysfunction. My last eight ball was the man I had just left at the subway. Years earlier, my colleague Emily had been prepping a narrative short film titled *Picnic Table,* and had asked me and Paul to serve on her crew. We spent a long day together in a dingy casting facility in midtown Manhattan where Craigslist hopefuls struggled to charm their way into an unpaid acting gig. It was as grim as it sounds. We subwayed back to Paul's Park Slope apartment afterward and started drinking whiskey. I am not a whiskey gal. I despised the taste, but my brain recognized it as alcohol and thus a liquid to be consumed. My weapon of choice was always white wine—pinot grigio or champagne. Not quite as cool as whiskey, I know. But that night I decided to follow along with the crew and watch John Ford's *The Searchers* while drinking a tumbler full of Maker's Mark.

At some point, the whiskey started to turn my skin warm and made Paul look like he was my type. I decided quickly, then and there, that it was a good idea to sleep with him. On day one of the project. The next morning, I felt far less confident in the quality of said decision. As we were doing the sheepish let's-put-our-scattered-clothes-back-on dance, we agreed that we would go to breakfast. We got to the bagel store and I mumbled a passing joke that he should pay for my bagel as he had been given my ultimate lady gift the night before. Fortunately, the awkwardness gave way and we were able to talk and find some commonality.

Paul was my age, twenty-four, and a video editor by trade. Lately he had gotten knocked off course and forced into a gig where he had to spend eight hours a day taping demo reels for third-tier actresses. He used to date a beautiful woman, but had been single for a couple of years. He decided to get back in the game and was looking for his next girlfriend.

Anyone who has been single for more than a week knows what a slog dating is. I was done with the merry-go-round and thought it might be a good move to try this whole monogamy deal. We started dating in January and formed a relationship based on a mutual love of simple pleasures, like pop culture and football. He was smart, funny, and could make a mean batch of spaghetti carbonara. I thought I had found my dude. My dad and stepmom were thrilled by the match—I typically dated out-of-work musicians, and Paul seemed like a guy who had his head on straight.

That summer I was staying in a windowless box of an apartment near Paul's place. In the summer heat, the $700 a month I was paying felt like at least $400 too much. After Paul and I had been dating for six months, he asked me to move in. I was tempted by the idea of saving a shit-ton of money by combining our rents.

I called my dad for his input. While he was not an old-fashioned kind of guy, I wasn't certain how he would react to the idea of me living with a boyfriend. After I ran the idea by him, he simply and emphatically said, "Do not do this. You are not ready." He told me that if I valued the relationship, that I should wait another year or so before making such a significant move. I listened, and then ignored him.

I moved into the apartment that Paul shared with three other roommates. It was a homey and warm house, filled with people who liked one another. I would soon find out that the only person in the house that Paul had a problem with was himself.

As soon as the locks clicked behind me on that first night, a different Paul emerged. I learned about his hatred of his job, his life, the people that walked in front of his car as he drove us both to work. In truth, I, too, had parts of myself I would've preferred to keep hidden. I was living with someone, and my freedom was gone. No more casual flirting with people outside the relationship, something I had done often in the past.

I started avoiding Paul, staying late at work while he would sit at home. I would often come home drunk, not having much to say to him. I felt stifled and he felt ignored, a toxic combination.

After being together for ten months, I decided to bring Paul to Dad and Jill's for Christmas. It was shocking for them to see how quickly his mood could shift. He would go from polite and talkative to someone who berated me for sport. I returned the favor with firepower, in front of them. When we had both had enough, Paul went outside into the backyard to smoke some weed. I apologized for his behavior, saying he had just quit smoking cigarettes and was "really tense." My dad narrowed his eyes, and said, "Be careful."

A couple of months later I started working on a longer documentary project that required some travel to L.A. I was prepping for an interview when I got an email. It was a forwarded message of a months-old email exchange I'd had with my friend Marc. He had sent me a bare-chested picture that showcased a new tattoo. I responded positively to the tattoo and to his body. Paul had found the flirty email on a tablet I had thoughtlessly left behind. I called Paul immediately and started with a falsely chipper voice, "Hi, babe, how are you?" He immediately told me to check my email, and I heard a click. My phone beeped and I had a new text message: a simple "fuck you" glowing on the screen.

The jig was up. I had been found out. It wasn't exactly cheating, but it was behavior that Paul would not tolerate. I wondered if he was going to kick me out. Did I even care? We had another pressing issue: He was supposed to visit me in L.A. in twenty-four hours. Soon he canceled his flight and forwarded me the confirmation. Message received.

More bad news came. The next day my dad called to tell me that his father, our papa, was in critical condition and likely to pass soon. I needed to get on a plane to Minnesota immediately. I was shaken by the news, as death was not something I had any experience with. I was about to learn.

The funeral was Irish Catholic, full of both tears and raucous laughter. A smattering of our strongest male cousins were asked to carry the coffin, and much to my dad's chagrin, I was asked as well. I was apparently the most masculine of the female cousins. As I helped carry the coffin, the weight of it and the situation allowed me to step outside myself and put the drama with Paul into perspective. After the burial I asked my dad, who was always a crier, how he was holding up. "He had a good ol' life and it was time for him to go." My dad was sad but he knew that death was always the ending that life had in store for us. He also knew a good death was never guaranteed. When my dad was forty-eight, his sister had died from an aneurysm. He'd wept for months, long enough to remember that things could always be worse.

I flew back to New York after the funeral and was surprised to find Paul waiting at the airport to drive me home. I had sent him my flight information on the off chance that he would come pick me up, as was tradition, but I wasn't sure if he would show up.

We drove back to our shared apartment in silence. The death in the family had given me a life preserver for the relationship, and I had to decide if I would take it. I felt conflicted, so I kept treading water. I wanted the comfort of a relationship, but none of the work or sacrifice. I soon realized that we had both picked poorly. Paul was a jealous person, and I was quite adept at making him jealous.

The explosion—or implosion, depending on how you look at

it—happened one night when Paul asked me to get drinks after work with some co-workers. We spent the evening laughing and having fun, doing that smug dance that people in relationships do around single people, but something about that fourth glass of wine made me want to act out. We got in a cab. I started texting a guy friend and flirting. I had changed his name on my phone to Liz H, a female friend of mine. I felt a little guilty but was able to quickly reframe it in my mind by insisting that Paul's jealousy made me behave this way. But it was all fairly obvious and Paul guessed the true identity of the contact, which quickly led to a shouting match. We were standing outside our apartment when he pushed me down to the ground. I looked up at him, shocked. "You pushed me!"

"You fell," he muttered in disgust.

We moved inside the apartment, where we continued to scream and rail and slam doors. He said the things that men say when they want women to feel small and useless. He threw my phone out the window. I told him I was leaving.

Unfortunately, that wasn't the last night of the relationship. But it should have been. We were still living together when I started seeing someone else, to be as deliberately hurtful as possible. I wouldn't come home some nights, leaving Paul to wonder where I was, who I was with. When I told my dad what had happened the night Paul shoved me, he said, "You need to move, and now." I told him that it was an accident and I had driven Paul to this point. My father was resolute, but he would not help me move. This was my burden to bear. I found a friend who was also looking for a place to live and began the slow, painful process of moving out.

In the meantime, my dad told me that he was going to call Paul to "set him straight." I begged him not to, explaining my embarrassingly bad behavior within the relationship. I felt like the whole situation had been blown so far out of proportion. Or had it just escalated so quickly that it was difficult to believe what was happening? Either way, I knew something irreversible had happened when the fight turned physical. Neither my dad nor I acknowledged that he himself knew what it was like to push a woman, that he recognized Paul's situation more than my own.

Much to Paul's credit, he picked up the phone when my dad called. He apologized, knowing full well that the damage was already done. He helped me move out and dropped me off in my new apartment. Even though the relationship was a flawed one, I felt scared and alone when he said his final goodbye.

I left it to my former roommates to take care of Paul while I worked on building a new life for myself. A friend of mine had moved into the house during that turbulent time, and I found out that she and Paul had begun spending more time together. I liked her a lot; she was wry, smart, stylish, and my physical opposite. I grew anxious and jealous of the idea that they might sleep together. I wrote to her in a panic asking if my fears were true or if they were an invention of my mind. She took some time and wrote back to me. I opened her email at work and started shaking. She admitted that they did have feelings for each other and they'd already acted on them.

I had not expected this. A raw anger took over. I knew I was finally getting a taste of my own medicine, but I was unable to accept it. Seething, I wrote back.

And just so you know, at the end of the relationship Paul became deeply scary and hurtful, calling me every name he could think of and then pulling a 180 and begging me to stay with him, that he was terrified to be alone, even became physically threatening one evening. I sincerely hope he never repeats that behavior but it is something he is capable of (I know he really regrets this). It's sad that it has gone this way and it's too bad that I lost a friend over it. There will come a time when the Paul thing falls apart (because trust me, no one who hates himself the way he does is meant to be in a relationship at this juncture in time) and you will want to talk to me. Don't. I am very into setting emotional boundaries for myself and I have deleted you from my phone. Please do not contact me.

Years later, I now realize how fucking hypocritical I was being. But at the time, I was wounded. The new guy I had started seeing broke it off with me, saying, "You are great but you have some issues you need to work through." He told me to call when I was ready. Instead, I called my dad over and over, seeking guidance, admitting that I had handled everything wrong, wondering how to feel about another failed relationship and the fact that Paul had moved on so successfully.

His responses were always solid and sound and made me feel better.

Dolly, he was a significant person in your life, but sadly not a significant person. His quiet rage at the accomplishment of others, his inability to take action in his own life, professionally and emotionally. She will know him as you now know him. Do not give either one of them the satisfaction. Seriously honey, he was the best 180 pounds you ever lost. Life is long.

I printed out the email, stared at it, and for the first time in a long time, felt that I could breathe.

16

The Criers Get Nothing

Click, Print, Gun, my piece about Cody Wilson, the 3D-printing assault weapons guy, was a success. In the first week of its release on YouTube, five million people viewed the twenty-seven-minute film. Those were insane numbers for a movie that long. VICE was pretty happy. It was another way for their brand to be seen as close to the zeitgeist. I was thrilled beyond measure and stayed up the night the film hit the Web to count the views hour by hour. Virality was intoxicating, and it felt like my work getting noticed in a big way.

When Stephen, a rival producer from a competing tech website, direct-messaged me on Twitter and asked to meet for a drink, I immediately responded in the affirmative. I didn't want to leave my job at VICE, but I knew my money situation needed improvement. I said as much to Stephen at the bar and he encouraged me to send an email of inquiry to the head of the site. I did, and the editor responded, inviting me to come in and meet with him.

I left my desk at VICE in the middle of the day, citing female problems, and took the train into Manhattan. I used the travel time to run through the conversation my dad and I'd had about money one more time.

"How much do you make now?" he'd asked me quickly. I had

gotten a raise in the last year and was up to $40,000, but I was still running at a deficit. "Forty thousand. It isn't enough, considering student loans and rent." He knew this much; I had been complaining about what VICE paid me for years.

"What do you want to make?"

I had never been asked that question. I paused and said in a questioning tone, "Sixty-K?"

"C'mon, we can do better than that. What about seventy-five?"

"Yeah, that would be incredible."

"Ask for that and see what they say."

Within two weeks I had a job offer in hand with a salary of $80,000; they had added the $5,000 to seal the deal. I was elated. I was flying back from a video shoot at a Bitcoin conference when I emailed my best friend, Yunna, with the good news. She matched my excitement but then said, "I think a change is absolutely the right move. VICE has never been that healthy for you."

"What do you mean?"

I could feel her thinking as she slowly typed out the next text message. "I mean, I think working there makes your drinking issues worse. Am I completely out of line in saying this?" I was irritated at her for bringing up such an embarrassing subject on the heels of my happy news. I swiped left on the conversation to delete it permanently, and we didn't talk about it again for quite some time.

I left VICE the only way I knew how: loudly. I told them it was because of the money. It *was* about the money, but also because I would always be viewed as "David Carr's daughter" there, a title I both treasured and resented. There was also the matter of inadvertent sexism. After *Click, Print, Gun* premiered we had a company-wide meeting. I had a feeling that Shane, one of the heads of the company, might give the film a shout-out. When he did, I was thrilled. He then put his arm around me and in front of my entire company said, "Who knew this little girl could do it?" It was a bewildering thing to hear and I didn't know how to react, so I smiled through gritted teeth. I wasn't an accomplished video producer with many millions of views under my belt; I was a little girl and they were surprised by my talent.

When VICE didn't match the other offer, I gave my two weeks' notice. Eventually an exec who I had worked with for years tried to woo me back with a counteroffer that was $25,000 less than what I would be making at my new gig.

"I don't think that is going to work."

"I would think about that," he said.

I stared back at him, silent but waiting for whatever came next. I expected him to tell me we were a family, and if I stayed, my growth at the company would continue. Instead, he chose a different route, a classic tactic.

"Just so you know, you are nothing without VICE. My guess is you'll fall flat on your face."

Jesus Christ. Every single part of me wanted to say *Fuck you,* but I heard my dad's voice, and I knew, without hesitation, that was not the way to end it.

I smiled and said, "I'll get back to you about your counter," and left the room. I went to an empty edit bay. Did he really just say that to me? Could it be true?

A week later I showed up at my new company, filled with optimism. I had earned my place there on my own. I had a clean slate, and I was going to take full advantage of it. I introduced myself at reception and was met with a puzzled look. I asked if the editor of the site, the guy who'd hired me, was there. "Not yet; let's see who you can talk with." I had no desk, no boss, and I was pretty sure no one knew why I was there or who I was. Not a great sign.

It got worse a couple of days later, when I was told that my first project would be to produce video for a Web series branded by a car company. Even as a fairly green producer, I knew that this was not good news. I'd traded a gig full of artistic and personal freedom at VICE to now make "branded content"—two words that should make anyone shudder.

I felt trapped and acted accordingly. All of the good advice my dad had given me fell by the wayside in my rush to find a place to stand. Things like "Don't be the first to speak; listen to the room" no longer applied. I thought I knew better. I thought it was my job to change up the video priorities at the company. Turns out, it wasn't.

VICE had a "Work hard, play hard" ethos that gleefully went to extremes. That was likely what Yunna was smartly referring to when she said it wasn't the right environment for me and my drinking. Party as hard as you want—no one will notice or remember your antics because they are all equally blasted. That wasn't true of my new surroundings, where they definitely noticed.

A couple of months into my new gig, I was in St. Louis on an all-day shoot. After we wrapped I went out with the crew and proceeded to get wine drunk, which led to my slowly but surely blacking out. I woke up the next day with little memory of what had happened the night before. I called Matt, a co-worker, and asked him what our start time was that day. He asked to meet me downstairs. I splashed cold water on my face and headed downstairs.

Matt met me with coffee and asked me to sit down. "Are you okay?" My painted-on smile faltered. "Yeah, a little too much to drink last night, but I'm ready to get back into action and get started shooting today."

He visibly cringed and said, "Oh, Erin."

"What?"

"You broke the camera last night. Don't you remember?"

In that instant it all came rushing back to me. The wine at dinner, the loud car ride home, ordering more wine at the hotel. The camera falling off the table. I had gotten too far out of pocket. No one else had been drunk.

I scrambled out of the lobby in a fit of embarrassment, telling Matt I had to make a phone call. The other producer on the shoot texted me and asked if I could run and get a hard drive, as I had a rental car. I replied, "Yes, of course." I was on the edge, but I knew if I could just finish a task I would feel better. But where the fuck was the car? I don't drink and drive as a rule, but I was out of it just enough to not remember where the car had been parked by someone else. I couldn't ask Matt and look like even more of a mess. I got down on my knees in that godforsaken parking lot and asked the universe for help. But the universe didn't answer, so I chose the next best thing.

"Hey, Dad."

"What's up, Dolly? You sounded blue in your voicemail."

I cut the bullshit and dove headfirst into the situation.

"I . . . it just isn't going well here. I can't control my drinking on shoots and it got out of hand last night." I explained the sequence of events, as much as I could remember. I felt panic rising in my chest even as a wave of relief crashed over me. I had put words to the secrets I had been keeping within me.

He listened carefully and then responded: "Listen, I'm really sorry you are going through this. It sucks and I have been there but you need to establish firm boundaries. No drinking on shoots, and honestly you should probably take a break from it altogether. Ask your co-worker where the car is, get the drive, and drink a fuck-ton of water. And then remember you don't have to live like this."

I knew he was right, but it wasn't what I wanted to hear. Who gives up booze at twenty-five? I felt like there had to be another way.

At the end of the day I sat in my hotel room and wrote down a list of promises.

1. I will not drink on shoots.
2. I will stop crushing on my co-worker and putting him in an uncomfortable position.
3. I will listen and watch how they do business here and determine a way to insert myself into their organization.
4. I know how to make great videos and I will show them as such.
5. I will turn this around.

I returned to New York and headed into work with a new resolve. Each day I flip-flopped between this place of new determination to get the job done well and responsibly, and thinking about what a fuck-up I was. I could not get that moment when I was reminded about the broken camera out of my mind. I would fight to shake it off and boot up version 2.0 of my working self. I showed up early, responded to work emails at all hours of the night, and constantly focused on developing fresh ideas. Slowly, I felt a shift taking place as a result of cutting back on my drinking.

I started working on a film about a topic I knew very little about but which fascinated and horrified me. Having been fed a cultural diet of *All the President's Men,* I felt a growing sense of excitement to do work that felt meaningful. Evidence showed that numerous Iraq and Afghanistan vets were coming back from tours with mysterious illnesses, so we traveled across the United States, interviewing soldiers, lawyers, state representatives, and finally a rep from the U.S. Department of Veterans Affairs.

I brought the tape back to the edit suite and started combing through the footage. I got pushback from Tim, an editor at the site, about my outline, and I asked him for a meeting. He moved up the time and said we needed to talk right away. I had met Tim before. He was handsome in a bookish way, but also a John Hughes–style jerk—the kind of guy who did push-ups while reading *The New Yorker* and bragged about it offhand. A real caricature but someone who was above me in the pecking order. We didn't exactly get along.

I walked in and took a seat on the couch. He stood, stared at me, and said, "I don't think you should go on the next shoot. I think you should focus on what is in front of you."

"I can do both."

"Yeah, well, this is not a suggestion. I am unsure about your ability to manage your time and basically your work ethic overall." He started to check emails on his phone as he added that he was unsure how long I would be staying at this job.

I was shocked. Sure, you could question my intelligence or storytelling ability, but my work ethic? No way. It was as if he had pinpointed the thing that would throw me the most off-balance. "I am sorry you feel that way. But I'll be fine." I turned and left the room, narrowly escaping before the tears arrived.

I sent an email to my dad.

To: David Carr
From: Erin Lee Carr
Date: 09/10/2013
Subject: Ran into some serious trouble at work

——————————————

I drafted an outline of the soldier doc and I kept feeling intense and harsh criticism of the draft from the features editor (written editor) of the site. He called a meeting today to discuss and get it out in the open and see how I could fix the problem.

He told me he is worried about the piece and ultimately my work at the site and that if past videos are any indication of what my work looks like i wont last long. he is not my boss and is only one person. I spoke with Stephen and he said we had to call a meeting. that i was brought in to do my version of video and this guy is actively causing me to not be able to do that.

How to proceed?

My dad told me to call him at his desk and he talked me down off the ledge. The next day I received this email:

My money, smart money at that, is on you, this week and always.

Making great content is hard. Making change is harder still

Dad

I didn't go out on any shoots and instead stayed in New York and worked on the documentary. I knew this one needed to be strong for me to hold on to my job. We finished the piece. My gut told me it was good. I slept for what felt like the first time in a week, crawling into bed after sending the link to the powers that be with the finished film and crashing for nine hours. When I woke up there was a text on my phone from Tim, asking to meet to discuss the piece.

I went into the meeting feeling confident. Tim sat across from me at the conference table and looked down at his notes with his Weezer-style glasses: "One note. It lacks depth." The piece would need to be overhauled. I disagreed vehemently with his review but could see that the writing was already on the wall. My future looked even more uncertain a few days later when the head honcho requested a one-on-one meeting with me. I once again sent my dad a flare. He told me to meet him at the *Times* and to bring a notebook.

I saw him from a block away, smoking a cig and pacing back and forth.

"Hi, Dolly, how are you?"

"Not good."

"Listen, they are not going to ax you; it's far too early for that, but if they do this is what you say."

I took a deep breath, realizing that what he was about to tell me was going to come from his firmly established middle-aged perspective and not that of a twenty-five-year-old fuck-up. But I knew he had been a fuck-up himself, so I didn't interrupt him.

"You better think about what you are about to do before it is too late. You brought me here from a competing organization, a job where I was doing well, and you took me out of there. You put me in an organization that had no room for me, one that didn't even know I was coming. You set me up to fail. You need to give me a second chance, and we can work from there."

I looked up at him, his eyes so serious and filled with intent. I wondered if I could deliver such a speech and believe it.

"I'm scared."

"Yep, that's normal. Do not let them fuck you here, though. And above all else, do not cry. The criers get nothing."

I nodded while scribbling it all down.

"I am on deadline right now, but I feel certain that it'll be okay. Call me the second you get out of that meeting." He kissed me on top of my head, like he used to do when I was little, and said, "Go. Get 'em."

I walked back to the building with my head held high, propped up by my new plan. Tim smiled at me as I entered what

I would later learn was my firing meeting. It took them an hour and a half to let me go. At the end I repeated my dad's words and added some of my own. Fifteen minutes later, the editor of the site turned to his number two and asked if they could keep me. Number two shook his head incredulously. "No, this is her firing meeting." We shook hands as I headed out of the conference room. I knew it had to end politely if severance was going to factor in.

I picked up the five blazers I had piled at my desk along with the rest of my shit, put it in a box, and headed to nearby Bryant Park. I called my dad. This time I was sobbing. He told me to come to Jersey, but I told him I needed to go back to my apartment to have access to my computer to strategize next steps. I called him once I got home and we talked for hours that night, drafting an email to my now-former boss with a plea for severance.

I didn't swear or name-call but tried to speak honestly. I was fired for my own behavior (breaking the camera, clashing with management) but also because they couldn't figure out how to work with me. I also knew it was a dicey start-up situation, one where newly hired employees were pitted against aggressive managers who knew little to nothing about the nature of video. I felt livid toward the company and my boss, but mostly toward myself for screwing up such an incredible opportunity so quickly. My former boss at VICE, the one who'd doubted my abilities, turned out to be right. I was a failure.

They responded and agreed to the severance. The last line of the email my now-former boss sent read, "I know you will do great things, sorry it won't be here."

I felt a semblance of relief, though it didn't last long. I woke up next day with nowhere to go. I wasn't hungover, but I could definitely have eaten a whole pizza for breakfast. Humiliation ensued when I saw that my work email had been deactivated. There were only three emails in my personal email account, including this one.

To: Erin Lee Carr
From: David Carr
Date: 09/25/2013
Subject: honey

---

so, so sorry for the kick in the teeth. fucking hurts I know.

I am and have been so proud of you. you are smart, standup, tough and true.

this is ugly, but we have walked through plenty of ugly in our lives and we are still nascent, still rising.

I too, have confronted people who disregarded me, who underestimated, who wooed me and then screwed me. and they were all wrong.

there is a reason it had to be like this that won't be clear for a long time to come.

please know that you have my support—economically and emotionally—we will row together across this lake of shit and land on firm, welcome shores. I just know it.

I so love you and so sad you are hurting. you are a good person, a hard worker and a good journalist.

david

17

Sometimes You Get Both Barrels

When I was thirteen, seeking my dad's praise, I sat next to him each and every morning and labored to read the paper. I knew to opt for the *Daily News* versus *The Wall Street Journal,* so it wasn't that much of a struggle. I wanted to be just like him. And he wanted his mentee to be like the mentor. This, however, became less cute when I developed his biting, judgmental side and an inclination to remark on things I knew very little about. We were at odds when my character defects—quite similar to his own, really—began to manifest themselves in small and big ways.

The defects came to a head when I lost a job for the first time. My dad was in my corner, but that didn't stop him from being terribly disappointed at how it had all turned out. At VICE, I'd been doing work that he and I were both proud of. Now I was just another unemployed kid living in Brooklyn. But if he was nervous, he didn't show it. I got the severance we asked for and I thought a quick sojourn to our family cabin would be just the right medicine for the gut punch I'd received. I brought my good friend and partial-kissing-bud Derek and hit the road without asking Dad or Jill for permission beforehand.

I called them from the highway to ask where to find the key and how to open the place up. My dad went completely ballistic, yelling that I was selfish and an idiot, among other unkind things. Later, his former co-workers mentioned that my dad was no stranger to fits of anger and/or screaming. I feel like he tried to be less so with his children, but every now and then this deep rage would unleash itself.

I wondered if he was upset because he knew that some of my own poor behavior had led to my firing, and whether this cabin fight was just his displaced disappointment in me. I knew by this time that his mentorship yielded important results but his expectations of me, his kid, were far too high to be fair or even attainable. He wanted to change media, and he expected that if he put enough time into me I would be able to do the same. When I couldn't reach those goals, he yelled at me or, worse, ignored me. It wouldn't last for long, but it stung.

As soon as he started swearing on the phone, I told him I had to go. I couldn't take the verbal abuse after the week I'd had.

The next day I continued to feel panicky. I couldn't stand being in conflict with him. I needed him. I sent him an email to clear the air.

To: David Carr
From: Erin Lee Carr
Date: 10/11/2013
Subject: A couple of thoughts

Dad,

First I want to start off by saying that our relationship is deeply important to me. I care about you and am so grateful for the time, energy and knowledge you have bestowed upon me. That's why moments like last night greatly distress me. I will own up to the fact that I fucked up. I should have emailed or called in advance, like an adult, and asked permission to use the cabin and for details on how to properly open and close it. I did not do that. And for that I am sorry. But then we started arguing, you raised your voice and swore at me. I do not believe my behavior warranted that. You said that I am a bad friend and daughter, that I have my head up my ass. Instead of talking about the issue at hand, we went on to discuss my character failings within the family. I know that I have always been the "selfish" child, a moniker that I used to deserve. The argument we had last night made me feel so small and powerless, I know that you do not love me any less, but it sincerely broke me down in a way where I am already feeling so broken and like a failure. I would hope that you remember that I am human, that I am trying and that I love the family that I am part of. Jill told me that she is "marking this down," I hope that you guys have marked down the ways I have helped the family in addition to the ways I've let you down. I am sorry I couldn't speak to you on the phone about this. I, like other members of our family am better with written words.

I hope we can see this moment and move on in a constructive way. I don't want to restart the argument I just wanted to let you know how I feel.

To: Erin Lee Carr
From: David Carr
Date: 10/11/2013
Subject: Re: A couple of thoughts

---

honey,

selfish and giving, loving, funny as hell, smart and crazy making, you are my daughter, I adore you, am so so proud of you. and i love you. we want you to have good things, soft landing and all of it, but you made it hard this time around.

relax, kick back, enjoy yourself, and know that you are loved and
looked after. I am off to paris with deadlines crawling all over me, but
i very much like your New York Observer memo. beautifully done.

we will maneuver through all of this, together, in our imperfect ways.
sorry for your bumpy ride up, but enjoy the air and the lack of nyc.
we will talk more. (and the reason that you got both barrels is that
you took the time to condescend to me in the middle of an argument. I take that from no one, including you, so don't take it person-
ally.)

this is a bump in a great and growing relationship, one that I count
as treasure and lean on. I need you in my corner just as bad as you
need me.

i love you madly and truly.

david

That was the thing with my dad. In order for our relationship
to work, I had to learn to not take his darker moments person-
ally. Sometimes, though—very rarely—I would push back and
carefully explain to him that his expectations were out of sync
with reality. He just expected too much out of me.

Nothing made this more obvious than a trip we took as a
family a few months later. My dad was always one for big ges-
tures, and he decided that he wanted to treat himself and his
tribe to a weeklong stay in a remote village in Costa Rica. He
told us to dream of coconuts, salt water, and friendly monkeys.
Our family did not always travel well together. We all took turns
being at odds with one another, apart from Meagan, who pretty
much got along with everyone.

We arrived at Montezuma. Meagan, Madeline, and I would
stay in the casita, located down the hill from the main house
Dad and Jill were staying in. Day after day, Dad gave us our

marching orders and we'd often pile into a car that was meant to have four but was now carrying six passengers—my grandma was along for the ride, thankfully. One day I was nursing a particularly bad sunburn and thoughtlessly opened my mouth to complain for the eight hundredth time.

"It's so fricking hot in the casita."

"Erin," my dad started. He paused and stared at me through the rearview mirror.

"Looking at you is like looking into a dirty mirror," he spat out the car window. No one said anything. I had no idea what to say or where it came from.

Meagan broke the silence. "Dad, it is not okay to say that."

He grunted and got out of the car, and just like that I was left there, my mind repeating that sentence over and over. It felt like I had been slapped.

I raced down to the smaller cabin and sat on the bed, still reeling. I hated that his words had gotten to me, but even more so I hated that I could see truth in what he said. My mimicking behavior had led me to pick up his deficits as a human, and I was unable to see clearly enough to attempt to fix them. I would have to become my own person, but at what cost?

I mentioned to my dad that I had been invited to TEDx to speak about my documentary work. It was a local Brooklyn event with around thirty people in attendance, but it would be filmed. Due to a fairly memorable disaster with my high school debate team, I had a slight public speaking phobia. I sent a flare to my dad, and he came back with this manifesto:

I have some thoughts about ways for you to go. so thrilled by this. comes at a perfect time in your professional development. you won't be perfect, but you will be perfectly amazing.

some things for you to think about. . . .

storytelling still attains . . . and that means characters and import, but also editing and writing.

viral is as viral does. it can't be gamed, but it can be sought.

you are standing there as a kid in brooklyn who has trouble figuring out how to put together a bed from ikea, but figuring things out as you go is a plenty good way to go when the media business is reconfiguring itself.

the loss of legacy business model has been brutal for people who worked in it, but the absence of friction is profound. dad's first big story at 24 was seen by 30K, erin's 10M. see attached slide

there are many platforms and many are important. there is where you work, there is reddit, there is twitter, there is YouTube. they all infect each other.

you are more influential than you think. by citing the great work of others in your social media feed, when it comes time to pimp your own stuff, you have credibility sharing credit and sharing duties matters. great work comes from the spaces in between people. sitting alone in your room talking to a web cam or hitting the streets by yourself rarely yields excellence.

ppls want to see ppls talking to ppls. social medium desires social media. one where people are interacting.

not all the values of television are worthless. 70 year legacy has yielded some best practices.

sound matters, desperately especially on small platforms. people see stories with their ears.

short form requires guidance. you can't get people through a lot of stuff in a short amount of time without installing some signage.

we are in a great epoch of documentary film. many of the most important stories, the one that shake the world, often come from documentaries. cite examples.

what is beautiful on your television is not what is beautiful online. authenticity and verisimilitude are beautiful, not good hair and big heads.

the intimacy of the medium often requires more intimate, less distant shooting. we want to be near, we want to almost be in the picture.

you are not an intrinsically interesting subject. journalism, and that's what it is, requires you to leave your place of work or residence, go out and find more interesting than you and then come back and tell your audience about this person, place or thing.

hope this helps

david

18

Gut Check

"So gut checks all around and plans need to be thought through
and considered. The most important thing is a look inside.
What do you want and how bad do you want it?"

My dad wasn't the only person who had to deal with my joblessness angst. I spoke in equal measure to my twin, who had her own challenging job at a mental health facility in Detroit. While she didn't have media-centric advice to offer, she did keep me positive and cheerfully reminded me that things were going to work out.

My dad did not mentor Meagan in the same way as he did me. He was softer with her, gentler. When they talked, they spoke about their internal lives and how they felt. They had a closeness that wasn't performance-based.

While I often felt like a burden to my dad, with all of my SOS emails, my sister Madeline kept more to herself, letting my dad in only in certain moments. I think she was his favorite. Madeline, nicknamed Maddie, was quiet, thoughtful, and the queen of the one-liner. She didn't feel the need to prove herself to him, and that was a strategy that seemed to work.

I wasn't feeling particularly industrious on those nights following my firing. My brain, my perpetual worst enemy, kept reminding me what that VICE exec had said, that I was going to fail. He was right, I grudgingly had to admit, but would this failure dictate the rest of my career? Would I let some asshole continue to be right? No. I set out to find the next gig.

I asked my dad if I could come home and strategize with him. This was after our cabin fight, and we were having our issues. He was stern in his response: "Never ask to come home, just do it and let me know when so I can make time." I hopped on my least favorite mode of transportation—the bus—and made my way back to Jersey. He was outside on a work call, smoking his way through a pack of Camel Lights and tapping madly on the VAIO laptop he carried everywhere with him. I waved hello. He motioned for a kiss on the cheek. He raised his hand to signify he would need five minutes.

I set up camp in the kitchen, on the giant oak table that took up most of the room. I had already started surveying the cluttered media ecosystem and drafting up a list of people to reach out to for gigs.

He came in, wearing his headset, smelling mostly of cigs but also of coffee.

"So what can you tell me?" he started.

"I wrote up a list of people/places/things. I would love your feedback . . . if you have time," I trailed off nervously.

"Honey, I always have time for you," he countered in his typical fashion.

"Okay, here it is." I handed over my laptop, which was rundown and chugging loudly.

He took in the list. "Well, you are going to need more places than this. Let's cast a wider net."

My list was *The Guardian,* Al Jazeera, CNN, Mic, and my personal favorite, *Frontline.* "Put Chris Peacock on there, and David Carey and Andrew Rossi."

I dutifully complied and sent the inquiries out into the universe with no introduction from my dad. I needed to start the dialogue on my own. One email would prove to be particularly important.

Hi Andrew,

Congrats on Ivory Tower! I wanted to get your insight on a professional matter. I started work at a new company four months ago, leaving the red-hot VICE for new challenges and reasonable pay. Unfortunately, I situated myself at an organization that had no room for me. I saved some money up and told them it wasn't working. I am now searching for a better fit where I can continue to make good videos.

The business of documentary filmmaking is a tricky and constantly evolving entity. I am looking for my next gig at a media company but I also wanted to try and seek your advice on the matter. I know you are beyond swamped, but if you have any time in the coming weeks I would love to get a coffee with you and chat. I can come to you etc and will be as brief as needed. Thank you for any attention.

A couple of hours later I received a response:

Ugh, that sounds like a frustrating course of events. But maybe it will create the opportunity to strike out on your own and direct your first feature? Lets get lunch, maybe next week on Wed or Thurs? I'm in Williamsburg. . . .

I was surprised by his quick response, and I wondered if it was because of his relationship with my dad. Andrew had spent some serious time with him, filming him over the course of a year for his critically acclaimed film *Page One: Inside the New York Times*. My eyes zeroed in on his line about making a first feature. I wasn't anywhere close to being able to finance that kind of thing. I needed a job and money coming in, and health insurance. Yet something about the optimism and casualness of the response made me feel excited about the meeting.

Andrew met me at a trendy Williamsburg restaurant. I started filling him in about my work life, keeping the details about my "leaving" my job sparse. I eventually launched into my plan of attack.

"I'm thinking about gunning for *The Guardian* or *Frontline*," I said. These two places offered some structure that I felt I might need. "What do you think?"

He said, "I think you should make your own movies."

I paused for a moment and then went on to explain the financial aspect of my situation. "I don't know how plausible that would be. I've only ever known and thrived in Web video and I'm not sure if that would translate."

He remained undeterred. "At those types of organizations, they will place their structure on you versus you creating structure. You know and understand story."

I had invited Andrew and his wife, Kate, to a screening of *Free the Network,* my first produced short at VICE about young Isaac Wilder and his quest to bring the Internet to Occupy Wall Street. We chatted at the event, but I was unsure if my film or I made a lasting impression on him. I guess we had.

We continued our discussion, and he asked what type of stories I was interested in. My world, at the time, revolved around science and technology. I asked him if he had ever heard about Ross Ulbricht or the Dark Web. There was a glint of recognition before he asked me to pitch it to him. Ross was a super-bright twentysomething who would go on trial as the founder of the illicit drug marketplace the Silk Road, located on the deep Web, also known as the Dark Web. Despite some nervous stammering, I made my way through it, and he said something about it being interesting to him. And then he said the magic words: "I could pitch this type of story to HBO."

Sheila Nevins ran the empire that is HBO Documentary Films for almost four decades. She was called the grand dame of documentary by *The New York Times* and could be described as bright, playful, and fairly aggressive. Everyone in the doc world knew and feared her name. Andrew had worked with Sheila when HBO acquired his first film, *Le Cirque: A Table in Heaven*. Sara Bernstein, one of Sheila's right-hand people, would also be involved in our pitch.

The exchange started off with an email in which Andrew asked if he and I could meet with them. I insisted on being in the room to pitch the concept, lying through my teeth that I was adept at pitching. While Andrew likely knew I was green, he also knew that Sheila and Sara liked working with women. I was excited about the possibility of being on the same email chain as them, let alone in the same room. They came from an unlikely class in media where women saw one another as assets, not competition. But I knew Sheila's and Sara's schedules were insane, so I didn't place much faith in the meeting happening.

On October 29, I got a call from Andrew saying the meeting was on. I immediately emailed my dad the good news.

To: David Carr
From: Erin Lee Carr
Date: 10/29/2013
Subject: rossi—update

---

he just called and said, "I hope you don't have plans for Monday at 2." He had Sara Bernstein, VP of Doc programming watch guns and now

Sheila Nevins will sit in on the meeting. He said it just got very real and not to talk to anyone about it. Just an update!!!!

My dad responded with a simple: "Wow. Wow. Wow."

The game was on. I prepped for days on the Dark Web concept and wrote up a ten-page treatment. I tapped a cybersecurity friend for a once-over to make sure it held up and then sent it to my dad with a specialized—for his eyes only—Google doc. I asked for his edits, though I really just wanted an "attagirl." Instead he asked me to give him a call.

"Dolly, you need to not stress over the language and structure of a document and instead focus on story. What is the human element for this? Why does it need to be made?"

I knew what he said made sense, but it was so much easier to control this document versus what existed between the lines. It wasn't the text that mattered, it was the story. He also advised having some backup stories to pitch. I had to scramble. I had only six hours to come up with some other ideas. He told me to think about stories that interested me, to focus on what I genuinely wanted to learn about. Check Reddit and Gawker, he suggested.

The two or three hours of research that I normally did before a meeting had morphed into a straight seven days. I had one shot. The more research the better.

The morning of the meeting I woke up at six o'clock and took a quick shower. I looked through my closet for an outfit that made me look the least chubby and most mature. A leather skirt and a button-up black sleeveless blouse. Tights of course—I always had trouble sitting like a lady—and combat boots. No heels for me. I needed to be in fight mode.

I arrived early at the diner outside Sheila's apartment building, where Andrew and I had agreed to meet before heading up to Sheila's. In an attempt to calm my nerves and appear casual, I ordered chocolate fudge cake and strong coffee. Andrew came in ten minutes later totally relaxed. If he was nervous, he didn't look it. Then again, why would he be? He had done this many times before. I paid the check and we headed across the street.

We took the elevator to a floor in the double digits. I checked the selfie option in my phone to see if I had any remaining chocolate in my teeth. Andrew eyed me curiously but said nothing.

When we entered the apartment Sheila was floating around in an oversized black wrap with matching soft black pants. She wore flats, and her silver bob was impeccably coiffed with a brown swish.

"So we have a proposal for you," Andrew started. "Erin has been thick into research about the Dark Web." He looked at me; it was my turn to take the floor. I opened my mouth and heard the words coming out. "I worked on a film about a man that 3D-printed weapons, named Cody Wilson, for VICE. The film resonated with the Web and I kept in contact. He told me he had a line in on an elusive character, Ross, who was currently sitting in a federal prison, waiting on trial."

Sheila looked at me with her brilliant brown eyes and said, "Nope, that is not the least bit interesting to me. Who cares?" I could feel a grimace coming on. Andrew looked unfazed as he changed topics and began to pitch something else. Fuck. Fuck. Fuck. I could feel my golden opportunity fleeing.

I stared at Sheila. She interrupted Andrew, turned to me, and said, "Your eyes make me nervous." I doubted this. Very little made Sheila nervous. I smiled in response and for the next two hours we discussed Christianity, circumcision, nuns, Russians, Warhol, mortality, and her dreams. I brought up a story I had read about in Gawker about Gilberto Valle, nicknamed "the Cannibal Cop" by the New York tabloids. Valle was an NYPD officer convicted of conspiracy to kidnap, rape, torture, and eat young women. The case was an unusual one. The defendant had never actually kidnapped anyone; he'd just thought about it and wrote about it in an online fetish community. A definite First Amendment rights issue. Now we were talking. I had unlocked some sort of interest in Sheila, and after one of the longest meetings of my life, it was time to hug goodbye. She looked at me and said in a teasing manner, "I don't like your ideas, but I like you. Andrew and you will make a good team. Bring me back something I like."

Turns out she did like one idea, because in the weeks that followed we were given a small development deal and the opportunity to turn the Cannibal Cop documentary into my directorial feature debut. Andrew was thrilled and said that it was a great meeting. As I walked away in the November chill, I felt electrified. Maybe my firing had happened for a reason. I called my dad and described the meeting. He said the words I heard so often but that had never felt so meaningful until that moment on the sidewalk in New York.

"Who knew? We knew."

19

Liability

"Remember. Eating b4 drinking. Sleep b4 rocking.
And measure twice."

While my career had righted itself, my drinking had not. Coming off my successful meeting with Sheila, I was excited to celebrate and share the news at an engagement party for my friends Will and Cary. I was one of the few former co-workers invited and I counted myself lucky to be included in these smart, chic people's lives. Had I always been sweet on Will? Sure, but who hadn't? He was that kind of guy. I wasn't worried about it, but I was aware that my drinking had been a little above and beyond lately, even for me.

After being cut loose from my job I had more free time than ever, and the wine was coming earlier in the evening than I cared to admit. As soon as the clock on my monitor hit six, an economical bottle of wine was produced from the fridge and drank in its entirety. Sometimes I would pour Yunna a glass, but more often than not, she demurred when it came to drinking with me. I drank five or six nights a week, always a bottle of wine or more. Wine calmed my fears about freelancing and the dark subject matter that I was engaged with on a daily basis. I knew alcohol was part of the reason I'd been fired, but I ratio-nalized it whenever it popped up in my brain—the broken camera, the hangovers. I knew sobriety was for "later," not now. I needed alcohol.

As I got ready for the engagement party I made the conscious effort to look myself in the mirror and say, "You are going to have no more than three drinks tonight; you are not going to do any coke." I decided to put an Adderall in my pocket to reward myself for keeping to three drinks. This is the kind of bizarre logic I resorted to. If I verbalized my limits I would sometimes adhere to what I had set out to do.

I met a mutual friend on the walk over and felt myself growing more and more anxious. It had been ten months since I left VICE, and this was one of the first times I was going to see some of my former co-workers. I was embarrassed to admit that I was no longer at the job that I had left the company for, and the development deal with HBO, while exciting, didn't feel very tangible. Nerves and a party had always been a toxic combination for me, but I pushed the feelings away as we made our way toward the venue.

The party was at a production company space that looked like a film set, full of stuffed birds and glass jars. The first half hour of a party is usually very dull, but drinking white wine helped ease the boredom. I stared at my hands and feet and thought about what made sense to talk about with other guests: the happy couple, the endless winter that we had been having. Suddenly and without consciously noticing it, I began to feel the effects of the three glasses of wine. I heard the men laughing next to me as I put my hand on my hips and grinned. I instantly felt more attractive as I went into the bathroom to reward myself for keeping on the three drinks train. I snorted the Adderall instead of popping it, deciding that it was probably best to save half for later.

There was a champagne toast and I was confronted with a

familiar choice: Say yes to another drink, or say no and stick to the plan I had set out for myself. I always chose the former. Whenever the question of to drink or not to drink arose, the answer for me was almost always a hard yes. I was unable to control or moderate my drinking once I had already consumed alcohol. I drank that champagne, my fourth glass of wine, in a matter of minutes.

That was the last conscious decision I made that night. The following details were told to me after the fact because I was blackout drunk at the time. I decided that it was time to make a speech about how I felt about the groom. I meant well, but instead of a quick, thoughtful toast, I rambled on and on, offering up flirty innuendos at Will and making completely inappropriate remarks, including saying I was jealous of the bride-to-be, but she was pretty hot, too. Eventually, after falling down on the dance floor for the third time, I was asked by a family friend to leave the party. One of my good friends and favorite drinking buddies, Kathleen, helped get me into a cab. I pleaded with her to hit up another bar with me, but she shook her head, begging off and saying that she wanted to go home. The night was over for her but not for me. I made the taxi stop at the bodega near my home where I grabbed a six-pack of tall boys, content to sit on my computer and drunkenly Gchat until the sun came up. Three drinks had turned into ten.

I eventually passed out, then woke up at noon to shooting head pains. I searched my bed for my phone to take stock of the previous night's damage. It was nowhere to be found. I looked at the empty beer cans and slowly realized what I had done the night before. A shiver of embarrassment worked its way down my spine. What did I do at the party? My memory of the night appeared to me in quick flashes, but the flashes were troubling. I needed to get in touch with Kathleen. While we saw wildness in each other, she would no doubt reassure me (as she had in the past) that my behavior hadn't been so bad. I tracked her down in a nearby café where she was having brunch with her boyfriend like a civilized adult. She had my phone. I was limping for some godforsaken reason, and when she saw me she immediately looked concerned. "Hey, you okay?"

I nodded my head as nonchalantly as I could, but I knew I was at some sort of breaking point. It wasn't that something horrific had happened; it was the simple and irrefutable fact that I could not control or moderate my drinking. I'd set a boundary for myself and once again had blown past it. I needed to try something different.

I crawled toward the subway. The shining sun mocked the deep regret that was setting in. I needed to tune out. I frantically searched for my headphones and discovered that the drunk version of me had jammed them into my borrowed iPad. Somehow I had broken my headphones and only had the jack inside. Ugh, what an idiot. My phone was dead, the iPad was toast, and I was alone with my thoughts—the thing I used alcohol to get away from. I felt like such a cliché, a bored mid-twenties adult who had succumbed to my genes. No amount of smarts, or history for that matter, had taught me anything different.

As I sat on the subway ride home, I knew for certain that my drinking was way beyond the range of normal. My skin was cracked and dehydrated; I didn't know what to do next. The answer, however, was obvious to my dad.

"You need to give it a break."

"For a week?" I countered.

"More like a month."

"I can try."

A month away from white wine seemed like a ridiculous amount of time to me, but definitely more doable than forever.

What I didn't realize at the time was that my dad, a member of AA, was twelve-stepping me, showing me a way out of alcoholism, one day at a time.

I went home and dumped out the half-finished bottle of wine I had in the fridge, along with the unopened bottle of champagne I was saving for a special occasion. I felt like throwing up while I did this, watching the liquid and dollars wash down the drain. I ordered the generic pad Thai from the restaurant down the street and hunkered under the covers.

Weeks later, a mutual friend of the engaged couple posted about the cute invite she had received for the wedding. I had already checked my mailbox for the day: nada. It was days later when I realized I was waiting for something that would never arrive. I emailed Will to finally apologize for the behavior and wreckage I knew I had caused. I received a blistering response, calling me out and saying it was time to take a break from the friendship. I completely understood, but I deleted it immediately, unable to withstand having the email even exist in my inbox. He knew the truth, and I knew it, too. I needed to try a program of recovery.

20

Ninety Days

I t had been ninety days since I got that email from Will, and something sort of magical had happened since receiving it. I had not had a single drink. I had become sober.

My life became routinized. I attended AA and therapy regularly, feverishly worked on my HBO project, and in my off hours hung out with my boyfriend's dog, Gary. After years of battling daily headaches, I had forgotten what it felt like not to be even slightly hungover. I felt like a superhero.

As a matter of AA tradition, I invited my dad, who was also sober at the time, to my ninety-day celebration meeting. It fell on the same day as my stepmom's birthday. I knew we would be having a big party for her the following weekend, one replete with a mariachi band and a delish taco truck. I definitely wanted him to attend this significant event in my life, and as childlike as it may have been, I wanted him to pick me. I signaled as much to him in a passive-aggressive exchange.

To: David Carr
From: Erin Lee Carr
Date: 06/04/2014
Subject: Better on email

Dad, thanks for calling me. I am feeling uncomfortable with saying this on the phone so email felt like a better bet, we can follow up and chat tonight but I wanted you to hear me out.

I am sure it was a hard phone call to make but it was a hard phone call to receive. I'm also sure it sucks being put in the middle but I just wish this had been handled better. I called last week and said that it would be significant if you could come to my 90 day meeting. You know as well as I do, its a big deal and one that I have fought hard for. While I totally understand why Jill's birthday and 50 is a big deal, you guys are having a big party on Saturday to celebrate it. I know rationally that my sobriety does not take precedence over anyone else's life but my own but this is something that makes me sad. Jill is going to have GG and Grammy Diane tomorrow, I will have no one as it is a closed meeting.

That said, I think it would be better if you respected Jill's wishes for tomorrow but we can chat about it.

As was his fashion, he considered this for a whole thirteen minutes before typing back his response.

To: Erin Lee Carr
From: David Carr
Date: 06/04/2014
Subject: Re: Better on email

———————————————

Very well said. Heard. See you there one way or another. Quick dinner cuz closing piece.

I adore you and love your ability to come to your own behalf. Tell me where to be for meeting. Looking forward.

He knew that he could not force sobriety on his kid. For most of the time he was parenting me, he'd abstained from drugs and alcohol. It affected the way I saw him. He had this secret way of living that protected him against the clear bottle and the chaos that it brought along with it. I wondered if I was play-acting. Had my drinking gotten so bad that I needed to totally abstain as well? Where did this fit in with my idolizing tendencies?

Before the meeting, we went for dinner at a local empanada joint in my neighborhood. We both ordered Mexican Coke and cheered to the ninety. I could tell he was curious to see if I would keep it up. I had made it past the month that we had first talked about. I caught him staring at his phone; he eyed me and put the phone back in his bag. So, what's next? he asked. But I had a question for him.

"Do you think I'm an alcoholic?"

He answered immediately with another question: "Did your life get better when you removed alcohol from the equation?"

I meditated on this while taking a sip of my Coke. Well, there were no hangovers. I was sleeping well. I could get to business meetings on time. My newish boyfriend seemed happier when I didn't ask him for the sixty-seventh time to repeat what had occurred the night before. My professional life and the HBO film I was making seemed fragile, at a bit of an edge. But the movie had not gone away like my job had. I said as much and he said, "Well, that seems better to me."

We headed over to a small room in a church basement in the old-fashioned Italian part of Brooklyn to mark my achievement. I can't say much more about what went on, per AA rules, but I had a big internal grin when he raised his hand to speak. If I was a betting woman I would have placed heavy odds he would pipe up; rarely did he leave a room unaddressed. I loved it, though; I loved hearing what he had to say about his own attempts at ninety days, how hard-won it was, and what it was like to see his kid get there. I didn't care if people in the room knew he was my dad. I was proud to be with him, and I felt lucky to have him.

Earlier that morning he'd emailed me the following note:

I have been knowing you for a long time, but I can't think of a time when I have been prouder of you. you go to 90 the old school way, crawling on sometimes bloody fingers a single day at a time

it speaks to your willingness, your seriousness and your humility. you have earned your chair, you are an important, vital part of the fellow-ship, and so central to my happiness and joy.

congrats on counting and piling up all of those one day at a times.

dad

all is well. writing. and listening to? The Pains of Being Pure at Heart. the ep. it's weird when you get alone time with your iPod and you realize that there is stuff on there that you love that you don't even know about. . . .

I like that you are being patient socially and looking after yourself. and in terms of being comfortable with the self, I struggle a lot with that. if something cool happens or I see something grand, did it really happen. watched meteor shower in the middle of the nite and somehow it seemed less valid, less cool, that it was only me and the dog. think it is a defect of character. but I have made enormous progress in being by myself and looking after myself. making good food that only I will eat, having little treats like This American Life that are mine and mine alone. . . .

xo

d

21

SOS

"Do the work."

In our household, when I was growing up, there was no TV allowed on weekdays, only books. We were going to be strong readers, come hell or high water. As a teenager I fell in love with movies instantly and read all the books on cinema I could get my grubby little hands on. Every Monday, I knew what went huge (or fell flat) at the box office that weekend and would often recite the statistics over my Honey Nut Cheerios at the breakfast table. My bible was *Entertainment Weekly,* and in a tribute I hung up my favorite covers, plastering every wall in my bedroom. When my dad invited Jay Woodruff, then assistant managing editor of *EW,* to visit my *EW* shrine, he said, "So this is what it feels like to be stalked."

In my ongoing obsession, I compiled a list of hundreds of movies to discuss with my dad. If they were rated R he had to determine whether my fourteen-year-old brain could handle it. I loved spending time with him in this way. From *City of God* to *Donnie Darko* to an ill-advised screening of Stephen Frear's *The Grifters* (which showcased a doomed love affair that involved incest and was a little too awkward to watch with my dad), movies were our thing.

My father always budgeted lots of time before the movie started (he was a freak about getting an aisle seat), and when we strolled up to the snack bar he would say the magic words "Get whatever you want." Giant buckets of popcorn (with plenty of chemical butter), a large fountain Diet Coke, and Sno-Caps—never forget the Sno-Caps. We would play a game before the movie started. We'd watch the trailers for five seconds before judging the film—would it be thumbs up, thumbs neutral, or thumbs down? We didn't agree; I was the harsher critic of the two, giving the majority of the films a thumbs down. I told him I thought the trailers felt watered down. He rolled his eyes. We agreed to disagree and had fun spending time together all the same.

Now the time had come not to watch a movie, but to actually make one and deliver it to HBO. I wasn't sure how to begin. My journo instincts told me I needed to get to the man (the assumed cannibal) at the center of the story.

Gilberto Valle had been found guilty of conspiracy to kidnap by a jury of his peers in March 2013. The prosecution alleged that this former NYPD officer had dossiers on sixty-plus women on his home computer and was looking up potential victims on the police database in his squad car.

But there was another side to the story. His defense team stated that he had never actually physically stalked any women. They argued that while the young police officer's thoughts and Google searches were terrifying, they were just thoughts, and he was within his rights to think them. The defense lost that argument, and Valle was sent to a federal prison in lower Manhattan. He was housed in solitary for his own safety. He was a former cop, after all.

In a matter of weeks I started visiting him inside the prison during Thursday visiting hours. He was lonely and bored and said he looked forward to our conversations. He even sent me a Valentine's Day card. The front cover had a single red rose. I emailed a photo of the card to my family.

Just in case I ever "go missing" you know where to look.

Erin

My dad's response? "I'm happy for the look into your world."

I remember getting that email and feeling a powerful sense of excitement. I had a world at which my dad was thrilled to get a glimpse! Most parents upon receiving an email like this would immediately press the "call my kid" button to put an end to this misguided quest, but not my dad, not this family. To move toward the darkness was a win, and it was something I would look to do again and again.

Months went by, and Gil and I kept talking on the phone. On my third visit to the prison, I stood in line, nervous, though not nearly as nervous as I was that first time. "Erin Carr?"

I stepped forward. "Yes?"

"You have been put on the denied list. Please exit the waiting room immediately. If you have an issue with your refusal you can call the Bureau of Prisons at this number." And just like that I was ushered outside.

I was never allowed back into the prison. No one ever told me this outright, but I could put two and two together. Someone saw that I was visiting an inmate that the BOP felt conflicted about, and so they restricted his access to press, most likely to hurt him and his mental state, or to keep something under wraps. I guessed that it was the prosecutor in Gil's case who pushed the reject button, though I haven't been able to confirm that. Gil had told me that he'd started to depend on me and our calls. This felt like more than a journalist-source relationship, and the Valentine's Day card confirmed that. The romantic inclination was one-sided, but I was anxious about how to handle the situation.

So I continued talking on the phone with Gil, trying to appeal to the warden to let me get a camera inside the prison. Each request was met with a refusal, and soon I was awake every night wondering if my project would fail and once again cursing myself for leaving VICE.

And then something pretty unbelievable happened. The same judge who'd presided over the trial decided there was insufficient evidence, and he overturned the conviction. This never, ever happens. After nineteen months—seven of which Gil spent in solitary confinement—he was out. Against my journalistic objectivity and better instincts, I was elated for him, his family, and his legal team. Clearly I was far from impartial, but I truly believed after viewing the evidence that he did not belong in prison. My film would reflect this perspective.

Once Gil was out, he started texting me constantly. He would ask about the specifics of making our film, but he also wanted to know more about me, where I lived, how I spent my time, if I had a boyfriend. I did. One day, I tweeted "my boyfriend sends me documentary ideas, swoooon." Within three minutes of the post, Gil texted me: "You have a boyfriend???" I knew then and there that he was watching my every move, online and in real life. To others, I reconciled the attention he paid to me by mumbling that it was because he'd had few friends since his arrest.

Multiple news outlets were targeting him for his "big" interview. I knew that if he consented to do even one of those, my project would be a goner. So far, he hadn't agreed to anything. I wondered if I had an opening. I texted him, asking if I could come over and film informally. He told me he didn't think it was a good idea and that he just wanted to focus on spending quality time with his mom and dad. I was disappointed, but I understood that he wanted privacy.

I was uncertain how to proceed. This was a delicate and dangerous dance. I called my dad. He picked up immediately and started asking questions.

"Hey, Dolly, so did you ask him?"

"Yeah, I did," I answered. "He says he'll do it but he needs space."

"Here's the thing: If you don't get that interview in the next couple days, you'll be fucked."

Blunt truth-telling is how he communicated with me and others. I hated that I knew he was right. I called Gil and convinced him that we needed to tape now.

I brought the camera, and Coffman, our editor-turned-shooter, began filming short handheld-camera interviews in which Gil and I talked about what it felt like to be set free. He was guarded yet playful. He invited me to his upcoming party he'd dubbed "Freedom Fest." He then asked me not to bring my camera. Okay, I thought, still a worthwhile way to solidify my standing with his family and legal team as he had other TV networks vying for his "exclusive."

I told my dad I was going, and he told me to be sure I took someone. I hadn't really planned on that, but it made sense. I asked my producing partner Andrew if he could go, and he said he could. I texted Gil and he responded seconds later: "I don't think that is going to work. I want it to be close friends only." He did not consider me a reporter, but a friend. I had two options before me: 1. Cancel, send a clear message, but possibly lose my in for the story, or 2. Go, and try to be clear about my boundaries.

I called my dad to have him weigh in. "Your call, hoss"—a moniker he gave people when he was pleased with them. He knew I had a conundrum but didn't want to influence me, as I was the one who would have to live with the consequences.

I chose to go. It was the wrong choice.

I took the subway out to Forest Hills, Queens, sweating due to the heat but also my nerves. Gil had first had to clear the party with his probation officer. It was just his family, his legal team, and, oh yeah, me. We ate in Gil's backyard; hot dogs sizzled in the July heat and were pretty unappetizing given the bizarre circumstances. There was enough food for twenty people, which made the fact that there were six attendees that much more conspicuous. About an hour in, Gil made a speech thanking each person for what they did for him while he was on the inside. I was second to last; he stated how crucial my presence was for him in his darkest times. The whole thing was next-level uncomfortable.

His lawyers' concern was clear: Was this girl going to be the liability that made all of their work go to hell? I am sure they worried about Gil getting confused and revealing something that they didn't want leaked to the press. That, or acting like a weirdo and crossing a boundary. I tried to leave early, but he cornered me for a hug and held on too tight.

Gil now started to amp up the creepy behavior, and I knew I would soon be at a crossroads with him and our relationship. One day while filming, I saw his eyes trail my cameraman as he went out the front door to get some exterior shots of the house. Gil walked over to me and started rubbing my shoulders, telling me how tense I seemed. My body seized at his touch, and I knew something bad was happening. I had practiced for this moment.

"Gil, you shouldn't touch me like this."

He replied quickly: "Don't worry, I touch my dog like this."

My brain and body froze and I prayed that our cameraman would come in and relieve me from this moment. He let go as soon as he heard footsteps approaching. This is when the alarm bells kicked in. Within ten minutes a car arrived to take me back to Brooklyn. I sent an email to my twin and called my dad and got his voicemail. I got home and cried in the shower.

Five minutes later my dad called me back. He had never been physically intimidated by a source, so he couldn't really advise in that capacity. Instead he used his network to connect me with Andrew Jarecki, a filmmaker he knew who had dealt with these issues specifically. Andrew had directed *Capturing the Friedmans,* a film from my early career must-watch list. Andrew also had something new cooking—a docuseries centered around a man named Robert Durst. That show would end up becoming HBO's hugely popular documentary *The Jinx.*

I called Andrew immediately. After some backstory, he told me it was about establishing a protocol. After our phone call, I came up with the following rules for myself:

1. Don't answer the phone or a text after 9 P.M.
2. If I see him, it is only during filming, and nothing that could be perceived as social.
3. Make it clear that I do not live alone.
4. If problems arise, have Gil's probation officer's number in my phone.

I look at this chaotic and, frankly, scary time in my life and think about how my dad reacted to it all. Was he scared or uncomfortable about the subject matter or the relationship?

> you are such a pro. what a great result. you are being paid. as a filmmaker. um. wow.

No, he was proud. Proud that he'd raised a kid who could go after these stories. Proud to jump in and help, either with some serious journo advice or a dark joke to lighten the mood—whatever was required at the time.

I continued making the film despite lingering tension between Gil and me. My dad urged me to be careful; the ego of such a man is a fragile thing. Gil had his freedom to lose but he had lost it once before, which made his actions unpredictable. That said, I needed to press him on parts of the story that felt deeply uncomfortable for both of us. That is what journalism is. It's what's lurking between convenient and uncomfortable.

The prosecution appealed the overturned conviction, but the judge's ruling held firm. Gil remained a free man.

22

Jelly Beans

"You are a rocking presence wherever you are, including in the center of my heart."

I typed in "Fahja," on November 16, 2014, and pressed the green button to call him. My dad had invited me to speak at Boston University, where he taught a weekly journalism course on media criticism.

I'd emailed him my presentation notes for the class and was met with a chuckle on the other end of the phone.

"You are way overpreparing for this."

"Better than under, right?" I countered.

He gave me very specific instructions on how best to get to his office from the Boston airport. I followed them to a T, but showed up to an empty office.

I threw down a heavy black messenger bag, jam-packed with underwear and cables of all sorts. It was the first time that I'd stood in an office that my father could call his own. His cube at the *Times* was a mess of books and papers. At home, he preferred to be outside on that screened-in porch that he often shared with the dog. I gazed at a couple of notes taped to the wall and wondered about their significance. I saw an ad for his upcoming class, and something colorful jumped out at me in the corner of my eye: a vat of jelly beans near the front of his desk. He never struck me as a candy sort of professor. Later on, after he died, I asked Madeline what that was all about:

> **Me:** Do you remember why Dad had candy on his desk? Kind of a Willy Wonka move, no?
>
> **MC:** Hmm, he had it on his desk because he wanted to seem approachable.
>
> **Me:** Approachable?
>
> **MC:** I tried to inform him that jelly beans were the wrong move.
>
> **Me:** What would have been the right move?

I heard his footsteps and tried to look busy. "There you are!" I got up to hug him, and in that moment, I felt a distance between us. I tried to quickly swat it away as I looked at him and asked for the Wi-Fi password.

We ambled over to his classroom. The desks were arranged in a hospitable square that made it clear everyone was welcome to participate. The students looked like me, if not older, and I felt the imposter syndrome creeping in. *Why am I here?*

After some chitchat, he introduced me. He outlined my résumé, and even mentioned my secret, that I had just finished directing my first feature documentary for HBO: "I like her but I'm a bit biased; she is my kid."

I blushed at this intro. I knew he meant for it to come off as charming, but it made me feel small. Like a kid. I shook it off and launched into how to find and execute stories for the Web and network. I found my groove, keeping an eye on him to sense how he felt about what I was saying. We argued about the pros and cons of using an iPhone to tell a story. His students jumped in, and we tried not to talk over them. I do not believe an iPhone is a substitute for a camera. He disagreed vehemently, saying that an iPhone is a tool many people have access to, and that I was being a snob.

When the class and banter were over, the kids lined up to ask me more questions. I fished business cards out of my messenger bag, careful to keep the Hanes underwear out of sight, though perhaps those were the perfect counterpoints to the snobbery charge. We headed to my dad's form of organized religion, the coffeehouse.

As we walked, I listened to his ragged breathing. *When will he stop smoking?* He looked different, older. Something welled up inside me. My superhero looked a bit worse for wear. He looked suddenly mortal.

I sat down and waited for him to begin. Being quiet was new for me. My dad sensed the change.

"What's up with you?"

"Nothing," I mumbled.

He had a cold so he headed back to the Buck (his nickname for the Hotel Buckminster in Kenmore Square), and I wandered the streets by myself. Later I crept back into the hotel and to my bed in the suite; it felt weird that we had to sleep in the same room. I heard him cough over and over again and wished I could put on *Gilmore Girls* to help me sleep.

The next morning, as was typical for us, the pendulum had swung again, and we talked easily. We rose early, around 5:45, to catch the Acela back to New York. We sat next to each other. I felt how I felt when I was a kid, excited to spend time with him and his fascinating brain.

Looking back, I get lost in these moments. Is the push-pull normal in any parent-kid relationship? I want to grab and shake my

*Digital communication was great, but
nothing beat the real thing that
traveling together allowed us.*

former self for being angry with my dad. I felt the tension of being both his kid and his mentee, one relationship always in conflict with the other. I saw his ambition and competitiveness up close and was disturbed by what they both did to his body. I was concerned by his appearance, the cigarette breaks he took . . . and now I'm haunted by my inability to say, just once, "Those will kill you. Please stop."

I could never say anything like that to him. He didn't allow for it. Now, all I am left with are photos and emails. But what do they say?

23

The Experiment

In the weeks after my trip to Boston, I felt a shift within me taking place. I had managed to pull off nine months of sobriety, but I wasn't sure if I wanted to stick with it. Was I really an alcoholic?

I had finished up production on *Thought Crimes,* my Cannibal Cop film, and no longer had a frantic schedule to structure my sobriety around. For months, I had been in hustle mode. Wake up, drink coffee, type for ten hours, watch a film, pass out. That fall, in an effort to educate myself, I made a list of all the documentary films I *needed* to watch in order to assist with the edit of my first feature. I became obsessive, always saying no to hanging out with friends because I had "work to do."

Truthfully, being around other people made me feel jealous. I hated going to dinner and watching those around me casually order wine. I would stare at the beads of sweat that formed around the wine glass and feel my mouth water. I despised that moment just before they decided whether to order one more, looking to me for approval, "Of course, have another!" During dinner, my friends' eyes would get a little darker and their laughter a little louder. A couple of times, they would repeat themselves. And all the while I am thinking, *When the fuck can I get out of here?*

So rather than put myself in that position and act like a jerk, I excused myself with "Sorry, on a shoot; let's touch base in a month"—as code for "not gonna happen." I spent night after night scribbling in a notebook about "structuring devices," and/ or points in the movie that bored me.

This is the time when I began to steal my roommate's Adderall, popping it for "emergencies," as in when I was too anxious to be stone cold sober at something. While it was true I wasn't drinking, this had essentially blown my sobriety. I was too ashamed to tell anyone, most of all my dad.

I had lost interest in the anonymous rooms where alcoholics go to find their people, their community, thinking that my relationship with alcohol was now different from theirs. Sure, I had lost a job and on occasion been asked politely to leave an apartment or party due to my antics, but I was just a middle-class white girl who enjoyed white wine and the occasional line.

All falsehoods I told myself. In reality, my identity was very much tied up with being the life of the party. After six months, I limited my AA time to one meeting a week, and then I stopped going altogether. I strongly believed that I could handle my alcoholism; I didn't need a room of cultists to tell me how to live my life. Instead of going to basements I read recovery memoir after recovery memoir, looking for easy answers. I was certain words would save me.

That was when I first read *Drinking, A Love Story* by Caroline Knapp. Finally, a girl who got it. Caroline was a high-functioning alcoholic who managed to hold on to a successful career in journalism and two misguided relationships all while drinking herself close to oblivion for fifteen years. The book's description of wine made my heart beat faster, and suddenly and without warning a craving would develop.

One night, instead of popping an Adderall, I chose to carefully pour the tiny beads on my desk and started crushing them into a fine powder with my MetroCard. I took a twenty-dollar bill out of my wallet and snorted two long lines. It wasn't wine, but I definitely knew I wasn't sober any longer. It had been a long nine months without a drink. I went down into the subway, and by the time I emerged, I was resolved to add alcohol to the mix, with the idea of "experimenting" with its reentry into my world.

In order to ward off this type of thinking I had kept a document inside my purse to read at just such a moment. In it, there was a detailed accounting of episodes in my life when alcohol had laid me low. I scanned the list and came to the decision that these were the acts of some other girl, some other life. I was confident that *this girl* could now moderate. I was sure of it.

Once, when I brought up the idea of moderation to my dad, he responded by telling me to look up Audrey Kishline.

I googled her and discovered a couple of things. Audrey was a woman who was convinced that the abstinence-only approach of AA was scientifically flawed. In 1994, she founded Moderation Management, an organization with a scientific, purpose-driven approach to reducing harm around drinking. Kishline claimed she was a "problem drinker" and not physically dependent on alcohol. It caused controversy and then a firestorm. In 2000, Audrey was found in her car drunk, with a blood-alcohol level of three times the legal limit. She had hit an oncoming car and killed two people, Richard "Danny" Davis and his twelve-year-old daughter, LaShell. She served time in prison, but according to friends and family she was not able to achieve any long-term sobriety. She committed suicide in December 2014. I knew all of this and yet I felt convinced I was unlike Audrey. Plus, I didn't drive.

After snorting the Adderall and heading out, I told my boyfriend Jasper to meet me at our favorite sushi restaurant in Queens. We had gone there every other week for the past year. Our favorite waitress came over and presented us with a dusty bottle of sake, a gift for the holidays. I took it as a sign from the universe. I carefully explained to Jasper my reasons for wanting to drink again. I pitched him on the idea the way I'd pitch a network or a media exec. I constructed my points evenly and asked for feedback. He seemed open to the idea. To be honest, I had been a pretty miserable SOB as of late. But he asked me to call my twin first. He most likely didn't want this to be on his shoulders alone.

I called Meagan.

"Hey, do you have a sec?" I asked her.

"Yeah, of course. What's up?"

I informed her that I was toying with the idea of drinking again—that very night, in fact.

"I need you to call Dad and or your sponsor and talk this through."

"No, I'm not doing that. I just wanted to let you know."

There wasn't much left to say after that, so the call ended shortly thereafter.

I knew I was putting her in a tough spot, but at least I had told her. I had gone on record with my decision. I didn't call my dad. This was a couple of weeks after I had asked my whole family to do a sober Thanksgiving for my benefit, and I felt pretty sheepish telling him all the insight and work he put into me and my program was for naught.

Instead, after dinner I rushed to the nearest wine store with Jasper in tow and picked out an upper-range bottle of sparkling rosé—no cheap stuff for my return to the game. Sake was never my favorite so we took the bottle home out of politeness, but my palms were sweating with excitement when I clutched the cold bottle of light pink liquid from the store. I realized we needed wine glasses and a corkscrew. Months earlier, in a fit of anger, I had asked Jasper to throw away all of our wine paraphernalia. Now I felt the magic that you get when you have a bottle or any sort of enhancer in your back pocket. I felt giddy in a way I hadn't in months.

When we got back to my apartment, I went to pop the cork and asked Jasper to have a glass with me. "No, thanks," he said nonchalantly.

I felt a flash of irritation. "This is important, just one glass." He reluctantly agreed, and I sipped the first wine I'd had in three-quarters of a year. The bubbles popped pleasantly in my mouth, and I felt the cool rush of calm immediately enter my brain. My body found it soon after. Forty-five minutes later the bottle was gone. I was drunkenly watching *Late Show with David Letterman,* but I felt uneasiness course through my veins. Why was I cooling my heels at home watching TV when I could be out? My mind thought back to the years spent weekend warrior-ing at Brooklyn bars from 10 P.M. to 4 A.M. and the occasional creepy apartments that offered access to more late-night alcohol. It hit me, as it had numerous times before, that I am not a normal drinker. The second I drink wine, I want more. I can't control my moods while drinking. I was able to rationalize it before, but the cravings were real. I was drunk again.

I texted Meagan and told her to tell no one about my decision to start drinking again, choosing to keep my experiment to myself. I got quietly drunk in my room a couple more times over the course of the next few weeks, having as much alcohol as I wanted, while I scrolled around on the Internet for entertainment.

A few weeks later, right after New Year's, Yunna invited me to happy hour at one of her gigs at Brooklyn Brewery. Very chill, no drunk assholes—it would be a perfect public place to try my experiment outside the confines of my apartment. She invited a couple of people, and a cool/sexy/queer girl I didn't know who looked like trouble showed up. I love trouble.

One drink turned into another. I was soon whispering suggestions about scoring a gram of cocaine. Since there was now a group of us, I rounded it up to three, just to be safe. My guy was called and we headed to my apartment, rowdy and full of excitement at the promise of the night to come. I put on Iggy Azalea's *Work* and set up line after line. A white girl copying another white girl posing something fierce. I felt the drip in the back of my throat, and everything became hysterical and lighter. These people, who I had known only for a couple of hours, began to feel like my best friends.

Yunna, my actual best friend, pulled me aside and told me it was time to go to bed. I looked at her wild-eyed. "Are you kidding?" It was three in the morning, and I felt just right. Two hours passed and the drugs began to run low. Someone in the group had a plan for the comedown. He offered me a Xanax. I swallowed it immediately and waited for the effects to kick in. When they didn't, I started to panic and asked for another one. He handed it to me and I crunched it with my teeth hoping that the drugs would soak into my gums faster. I finally passed out, my brain shutting off like a computer pushed into force-quit mode.

The next twenty-four hours do not exist in my memory. They have been recounted to me by my sister.

Somewhere in the back of my mind, while I was getting fucked up, I remembered that I had plans with Meagan for the following day. I told myself that I would call it quits "at a reasonable hour." That clearly hadn't happened. I partied through the night and apparently slept through the next day, missing meeting up with Meagan. She had called and my phone was turned off, never a good sign for me. She later came to my apartment to make sure I was okay.

"Yunna let me in and I went into your room," she told me later, her voice thick with discomfort. "You were facedown and the lights were off. I could see that you were asleep and I called your name. You didn't respond. I came closer and put my hand on your back and gently shook you. Nothing. I started to worry. I turned the light on and checked your pulse. It was slow. I had to decide if I should take you to the hospital or not."

After finally rousing me, she administered a field test to check my level of cognition, asking my age, how old I was, and if I knew who the president was. I did not answer her questions, but I did keep mumbling the word "shower." I could not walk or take my clothes off, but I kept saying the word over and over again. She undressed me and held me upright as the water hit my body.

I came to in the evening, having been out for sixteen hours. I noticed my sister sitting on the bed. I thought it was the morning; I was disoriented. In her most gentle voice she asked me how I was feeling. I was groggy and had yet to realize that I'd missed a whole day in the world. She told me she had to leave but that I needed to tell Dad I'd started drinking again. I nodded and said, "I know." Still, I was certain that I would never tell him the full details of what had just happened. There are some things a parent shouldn't have to know about their kids. It hit me that the experiment needed to be over.

I waited a couple of days before reaching out to my dad, ignoring the elephant of addiction in the room and lying through my teeth about being reckless. I eventually sent him an email.

Dad, I just wanted to touch base on something. You guys have been a huge part of my recovery so I wanted to let you know that I did drink again. I have been running on fumes for the better part of

9 months and work was a huge part of keeping me sober. When work died down I found it harder to have abstinence be my singular choice.

I totally get that this is crunch time and I am not off drinking in bars or being reckless. It's hard to be sober at any age but being 26 has its issues. I am not trying to justify the behavior or ask for acceptance but I don't want to lie to you guys. I love what sobriety brought me this past year. I needed time and space to determine what I wanted and the people I want in my life. Me drinking does not take those choices away but it does make me think hard about picking up the next drink. Thank you for your support in this matter.

His response, simple and clear.

Honey. Thanks for keeping me looped in. Let's chat this weekend and pls know I'm in your corner always. Dad.

He died forty days later.

24

The Water Has It Now

"Great work comes from the spaces in between people."

I spent much of the time writing this book at our family's cabin in the Adirondacks.

He wrote his book up here, too. The two of us lived together that summer in 2007. I was a waitress/bartender at a fancy-ish eatery down the road. The locals hated me for being that college girl who scooped up the seasonal cash and left with the tourists. I was nineteen and just about the worst roommate a debut memoirist could ask for. At the end of a long day, I would trudge back to the cabin, manage to grunt a "Hey" to my dad, and head into my room. I had plastered the walls with embarrassing emo band paraphernalia and would proceed to fire up a green bong that I named Jenny, after the nearby lake. I was *the worst*.

Pot was an innocuous substance to my dad. He didn't like the smell of it or the way I acted when I smoked, but he figured I was an adult and could smoke if I wanted to. How could he tell me not to? My dad had struggled with substances his whole life. Pot, coke, crack, vodka—you name it, he tried it. He is what one might call a garbage head. He was many things, but a hypocrite was not one of them.

After I was under adequate cannabis sedation, I would lumber into the kitchen and take root in front of the refrigerator. There I would stand for a good five to ten minutes, considering, through the different cooking equations, what could be combined to result in dinner. My dad would yell with irritation from the other room, "Erin, the contents of the fridge are not going to change. Close the fridge!" It was a tenuous time in our relationship. I didn't care about the intense crack addiction memoir he was writing, and he didn't care for the prolonged adolescent shift I was going through. But seeing as we were roommates, and family, we tried to find some ways to make it work.

I would hear him typing from every room in that wooden cabin. The speed and intensity with which he clanked on the keyboard were legendary. He would ask me questions sometimes about what I remembered from when I was little. Who was that guy that he used to be? Did I remember him? I did, but it was hard to put into words at the tender age of nineteen.

One thing we did have in common at the time was music. Not only our bond, music was also an education in taste growing up in our household. From alt-rocker PJ Harvey to the lyrical Magnetic Fields to the family favorite, soft-spoken busker Mary Lou Lord, music was a constant. When my dad introduced me to the supreme space pirate known as David Bowie, I was mesmerized. I had a tiny gray stereo that I placed right next to my bed, and every day for two years I woke up to the song "Five Years."

Teenagers, however resentful, are just looking for a way to connect, and through trial and error I had found my connection. I read countless books about the riot grrls, glam rock queens, and shoegaze heroes. I even went so far as to compile lists and make more than a couple of mixtapes for him. Making mixtapes for your dad is next-level dork. Yet that's what I did, without reservation. Liz Phair, Arcade Fire, Tegan and Sara, the Mountain Goats, and Against Me! were carefully organized into a playlist on my charcoal iPod. I usually put some Elliott Smith on there to round out the fun with some bummer. Dad got me very into the Replacements and Heartless Bastards in turn.

I sit here in the summer of 2017 at the cabin where he once was. I even presume to sit at his desk while I write this book, hoping some magical transference will take place and I'll be gifted, if only for this moment, with his way with words. I feel like a boy trying to fit into his dad's running shoes.

I walk down the shore along the lake and still expect my dad to be sitting there, propped up in one of our ancient beach chairs, our family dog at his side. But he is not.

For the most part, his belongings in the cabin have remained untouched. Books, scraps of paper with furious scribbling on them like "IBM" or "survival holding" sit on his desk. I laugh when I see his headset. God help you if you moved that headset. If you did, you were in for some trouble. On the wall next to his desk is a hodgepodge of objects: a flag with a Native American wearing a headdress with the words THE TRADIN' POST— ADIRONDACK MTS embroidered on it, a green sleeping bag that I am sure no one ever used, and in the center a silver plate with the words HOME SWEET HOME engraved. In the other room, empty cigarette boxes, loose change, and nails sit inside a yellow Frisbee. An ax and a hatchet hang on the wall in a *Shining* sort of way. A scorecard from Brookhaven Golf Course remains pinned to the post in the kitchen, documenting his first and last hole in one. Pictures of his wife and kids line the mantel above the fireplace.

What happens to all this stuff when a person is no longer here? The remaining objects are both comforting and devastating, compelling me to sit and stare at them.

I regret not going out on the lake more with my dad. He was

always asking, but I much preferred to be on dry land on my days off, curled up in the shade with a good book. The summer before he died, he cajoled me into joining him in the canoe. "C'mon, it'll be fun," he said as he pushed my shoulders toward the door. "Grab the paddles." I looked up, knowing that this wasn't a battle I would win. I dutifully grabbed the yellow paddles and chased after him down the dirt path. He kicked off his shoes when we reached the shoreline and then told me to hop in the front. I would be our guide.

Jenny is a small, quiet freshwater lake. It is stocked with fish, and no motorboats are allowed. My dad pushed the canoe out into the water and ordered me to paddle. We started to glide. I gazed out at the lake in front of us. We sat in silence for a while before he began to ask me questions about my life. How was it going with my boyfriend? What sort of things was he interested in? Always the journalist, he sussed this guy out based on what I had to say about him.

We moved toward the end of the lake and considered trying out the inlet path. I lied and told him I had heard it was too shallow this time of year. He mulled it over and agreed we should turn back. I asked him about his life.

"I keep thinking about all the things I want to do. Another book, maybe? But what to write about?" he said earnestly.

"Well, what do you want to write about?"

He paused for just a second. "Maybe Murdoch? I also would love to try and see if I could write fiction."

"You know you can do anything you want."

"Hey, isn't that what I am supposed to be telling you?"

We pulled the canoe up out of the water, and he made me put it on the rack. I protested because it's a known spider den, but to no avail. We walked up the path and talked about the time, years back, that he and Meagan raced up to the cabin from the lake.

An all-star long-distance runner, Meagan was the favorite to win. As they were charging ahead, he claimed she tripped all six feet one inch of him, and he went tumbling. I sincerely doubted that that had happened. While retelling the story, he mimicked the tumble and noticed that his wedding ring was now gone. He had lost weight over the past year, and even his fingers had shrunk. He hung his head and looked as if he might cry.

We both knew that the lake had the ring now. Sometimes the universe takes something, as if by chance.

My dad's last summer on Lake Jenny.

25

The Wake

"You are who you run with."

My dad had been dead for one day, and I had been given the onerous task of figuring out who to invite to his wake. Jill was tied up with their lawyer, trying to figure things out, as my fifty-eight-year-old father did not have a will. He had died intestate. I combed through my emails with him from just a couple of days earlier. I felt lost in trying to put the list together without his guidance—a feeling I would recognize thousands of times in the coming days.

Who would he want at his wake? I racked my brain for the people he loved, mentored, respected, fought and made up with and fought with again. This "fought" qualifier was important, as he argued with a great many people (myself included). And if you could come to the table, talk it out, and hug after? Well, then you were golden. I knew the obvious people—Sridhar, Ta-Nehisi, Tony, Michael, Fast Eddie, Lena, Erik, Sam, Brett, Liz, and Anthony. But who was I forgetting? I was bound to make a mistake. Only he would have had the power to hone the right list.

We held a powwow at our dining room table, which was covered in a simple silk tablecloth. I ran my fingertips against the threaded leaves embroidered on the silk.

"Should we look through his iPad for contacts?" I threw out.

Madeline was sitting opposite from me. Her curly blond hair fell down against her shoulders. Her eyes were cast downward, and all I could see were her eyelashes. She looked up, her eyes misty.

"No," she said firmly. I tried to explain to her I was not looking to steal emails but to plan this last party for our dad. She didn't explain herself but shook her head again. I fell silent and listened as I heard a car pull into the driveway. I automatically looked to the door, expecting him to walk through it.

I searched "Brian Stelter" in my own emails and found a mass email from my dad asking for some Twitter love about being on set of the AMC show *Better Call Saul*. I copied and pasted the addresses into a new email with the subject line "We Love David Carr! (Arrangements Email)."

On February 13, 2015, at 2:40 P.M., I emailed thirty-nine people the following:

You were so very special to my dad and if you can make it to the services in New York, they are as follows: Wake: Monday 2/16 at Frank E. Campbell Funeral Home (Time TBD but in the evening). Funeral: Tuesday 2/17 at St. Ignatius at 10am. My dad literally did a talk on stage last night before he passed. Always a worker, earner, thinker . . . he is incredible and we are so, so proud of him. He will be missed endlessly. Please contact me if you have questions.

Many replied with a kind memory about him, but the ever-present response was "Please let me know if there is anything I can do." I never had an answer for this. Others politely inquired if they could forward the details along or if it was private. That, however, was a question I had a definite answer for.

Please pass to anyone and everyone. He had so many friends. I
couldn't remember them all.

On the day of the wake, our neighbors Bonnie and Eric Baker
booked a car for us to travel in style from Montclair to the funeral home on Manhattan's Upper East Side. Jill, Madeline,
Meagan, and I arrived early and decided to head to a nearby
restaurant. No one had an appetite, so instead we split a bottle
of champagne. The glittering droplets, which should signify celebration, not tragedy, made my eyes hurt. I put a Xanax on my
tongue and swallowed, knowing I would be unable to take in
what came next sober.

We headed back to the funeral home and met up with Dad's
sisters and brothers, who had come from Minnesota. There
were smiles and hugs, but they soon vanished. One of the men
in black suits summoned us upstairs to see the body for the last
time before he was to be cremated. His siblings Joe, Jim, Missy,
Lisa, and John walked a couple of steps behind Jill, Meagan,
Madeline, and me. I turned around and could see my dad in
each of them, the same twinkling eyes. They'd lost one of their
own, someone they'd known far longer than any of us had
known him. We took the elevator a few floors up and were
greeted by more men in black suits murmuring, "So sorry for
your loss." I saw a funeral employee with a mustache and
thought to myself, *That looks terrible. I wish I could rip it off. I'm
angry at everyone, anyone.*

We walked into a softly lit room with wooden paneling. I
watched my dad's family closely. They had seen loss before; they'd
buried their parents and their sister in the past fifteen years, and
now their baby brother was gone. With grace, they knelt down
beside him and kissed him and said a prayer. They knew the order
of these things. After a couple of minutes, they left the room, giving us privacy. Madeline was the first to talk.

"But that doesn't look like Dad."

"I know," I said. "It's just so weird. It doesn't seem real."

"I can't," Meagan croaked.

Madeline walked over to the head of the coffin.

"Come over here. It actually looks like him from up here." I was skeptical that any angle in this room would make him look more like our dad, but I followed my youngest sibling. As always, she was right. I started to laugh out of nervousness, and they joined in, despite how inappropriate it felt. The laughter led to tears and we three sunk down next to the coffin. I clutched my knobby knees to my chest. I don't remember where Jill was at the time; perhaps she knew that Dad wouldn't want anyone to see him like this. She knew his wishes better than anyone.

We three girls sat beside the coffin knowing full well this would be the last time we would be in the same room as his body. We wanted to be close to him but not see him in that state. The men in black suits averted their eyes, but I knew it couldn't last forever. The service was about to start. The three of us took one another's hands as we got up and one by one kissed him for the last time. We took the elevator downstairs as the rest of his tribe began arriving.

Jill had lined shelves and end tables of the well-lit funeral home with Diet Cokes, pictures, and, oh yes, old-fashioned reporter's notebooks. You know the ones with the tan covers and the spirals on top? Version number 651. My dad bought them in bulk from the manufacturer, some genius in Virginia. I asked Jill if I could keep one and she told me she had saved some for us at the house. These were for others. I stared at her. Her perky blond hair had been coiffed, but her eyes were dark and steady. Lines creased her face. They seemed fresh to me.

After what felt like an eternity, it was time for the show to begin. A kind and gentle priest made his way up to the wooden podium, which was lit by a small brass lamp.

"In the name of the Father, the Son, and the Holy Spirit. My brothers and sisters, we believe that all the ties of friendship and affection, which knit us as one throughout our lives, do not unravel at death. God always remembers the good we have done and forgives all of our sins."

I leveled my eyes at the priest for bringing up the notion of sins so early on. I figured it would be a common theme. A baby gurgled behind me, which was comforting, and I tried not to zone out while the priest talked loudly about resurrection. *There will be no miracles here tonight,* I thought. The priest reminded us to be wrapped up by nine.

We had selected a few people to speak. Uncle Joe was the first to step up. His Minnesota accent was as loud as they come and unapologetic. He thanked the assembled crowd for being there and started out by saying, "It's tradition in our family—ya know, being so Irish—that we tend to celebrate as we mourn. An integral part of that is to invite people to tell their stories." He then launched into his own story with the simple line, "Do you believe in resurrection? I do."

I heard a couple of people shifting in chairs, but the room was silent otherwise. Even the baby understood that it was time to be quiet.

"As Father indicated, he was not a perfect Christian. Back then he was not a perfect anything." The crowd laughed, grateful for a moment of lightness. "Only exception to that was that he loved fiercely. Even in the throes of his crack addiction, he still loved us. But he made it hard to love him." The room was once again silent, the word "crack" reverberating. It was most likely not a word that was thrown around a lot at the posh Frank E. Campbell funeral home. My uncle, like his brother, pulled no punches.

After a couple of minutes, Joe stepped down and a familiar

face walked quietly up to the podium. My stomach tightened as I saw Dean Baquet, executive editor of *The New York Times* and the man who'd informed me of my dad's death. I knew my dad would be thrilled that he was there, but I felt deep sadness. Ever so meta, Dean started off by describing the email he thought my dad would have written him about his own obituary. He mentioned that it might be tart, and he would have liked it on the front page. Dean and the editors knew this and had factored in his wishes accordingly.

At this moment the overhead light was accidentally turned off. Dean continued to speak in darkness. He cracked a joke about my dad perhaps smiling at the fact that the announcement of his death on the site received two million page views. He spoke of the Twitter chorus that chanted at me after his death and recalled his favorites: one from Stephanie Mencimera, a *Mother Jones* writer who called him "a bundle of genius wrapped up in the unlikeliest of packages," and Politico columnist Jack Shafer, who called him "a master interrogator [who] used his guise the way an angler fish uses the wriggling growth on its head to attract and then devour other fish."

He said out loud that he wished he could share a recent memo about hiring that my father had written his boss, but he couldn't because "he had named names." And with that, I sat back a bit in my seat. For the first time all day I felt more relaxed. I was just listening to a story about someone who I could not stop thinking about. This room saw him as I did, fully dimensional. We weren't there to cover up the dark spots in his life; we were there to celebrate him wholly.

It was now time for people to come up and share any stories they might have about David Carr. I breathed a sigh of relief when the first was Erik Wemple, one of his longtime best friends who knew him as a boss, writer, and ultimately a kind of brother.

I watched him, blond and serious and without notes. He is one tough-looking dude who can also pull off a white cable knit sweater. Erik was responsible for clueing us into the beauty that is the Adirondack mountain range. The Wemples had owned a little cabin up there for decades, and when their family grew bigger, they moved to a better spot on the lake. My parents snatched up their old place and went about the business of creating their own memories there.

I closed my eyes as he told a story about our guy in his Washington-era days. My dad had battled necrotizing pancreatitis and was in the hospital when one of his employees, Dave McKenna, was set to have his bachelor party in Atlantic City. Never one to miss a party, my dad checked himself out of the hospital to attend the celebration and then promptly returned to the hospital after the festivities were over. The room erupted in laughter. He had *invented* fear of missing out, aka FOMO. Erik made sure to add, "He didn't miss anything in journalism, either."

His eyes fell for a second, as he steeled himself for what came next: a recounting of his own experience with parental loss. His own dad had died when Erik was thirty-one. "I realized that we as people never lose our need for guidance and for someone to play that role, and that's what David did for me. And just how David missed nothing, it is our turn to miss him. I will do that."

Michael Borrelli came next, almost as if my dad had arranged the lineup. I knew what he would say, but I could not wait to hear it. Michael represented another big puzzle piece in his life: striving for recovery. Michael waged his own battle with the disease, a disease many in the room knew intimately. A disease I had, but was trying to forget. I snapped out of my reverie when Michael said my name, recalling the previous week when we were called to the Montclair house to watch the Super Bowl. I came, as always, not for the sport, but to be close to my dad. To ask him questions.

"I don't know how many of you—well, most of you have probably seen or experienced David dance." He knew to pause, the big laughs coming loudly from all directions. "If you haven't, it's an amazing sight. I can't tell if he was the worst dancer I have ever seen or the best dancer I have ever seen. But he was the least insecure dancer I had ever seen."

Michael finished with a vivid punch line when he uttered, "And I was so uncomfortable." I closed my eyes and saw those dance moves in all their glory.

Ike Reilly was next, a musician whose songs I know by heart. Every word. He did not speak to my dad's career, because that's not what he knew. He knew him as a guy, friend, dad, human. "I really don't like being in this city without him."

Cousin Tommy walked up to the pulpit next. And then funny man Tom Arnold killed it with his talk of loyalty and ancient shenanigans. Dad and Tom had bonded over their mutual affinity for Minnesota and cocaine.

But something was missing. When would a woman get up and talk? *Should I say something?* Immediately, my stomach seized into knots. The long-ago-swallowed Xanax was no match for the mere thought of publicly speaking after these guys. I knew the order did not matter, but my dad would fucking lose his shit if I got up there and tumbled. It was time to be strong, insightful, tender. And funny. No pressure.

My Uncle Jim upped the dude quotient by speaking next, and to add insult to injury he opened by calling my dad "Davey," something he was not fond of. Once a big brother, always a big brother.

I texted my sisters to see if they were up to the job of talking about our dad. Madeline, ever the quiet one, can be a monster with words. Meagan is all heart and always finds the right thing to say. I have what one might call an inconsistent batting average. My sisters didn't respond. Nick Bilton was at the podium, describing my dad's last tweet.

And then my aunt Linda, married to my dad's brother and always a favorite of mine, made her way quietly up to the front. For a second she looked petrified, unsure if she was supposed to be standing there. I heard her laugh nervously as she recalled the family's confusion when my dad presented his book to them and told them the title was *The Night of the Gun*. Their father, my grandpa, had suggested the alternative title *Nuns Prayed for Me*. I grinned; I'd never heard that story. I'd officially learned something I didn't know about David Carr.

She motioned to her husband, John, whispering, "What was the other story I was supposed to tell?" Then Linda recounted her first meeting with the Carrs in Hopkins, Minnesota, forty-five years ago. It went all right, but she later found out that not ten minutes after she left, my dad was arrested in that very driveway. "Long hair, plaid leisure suit, he was just nuttier than a fruitcake." She cackled and so did I at the thought of him in a plaid suit.

James Percelay read the room and knew he should speak to the suburban side of my dad. Whether it was mowing the lawn or firing up the snowblower my dad always had a gadget or two to aid in house maintenance. He liked these simple tasks, and he bonded with many a neighbor about #thissurburbanlife.

Lena Dunham got up and said what I was thinking: "I thought it was important to come up and fill out the female contingent of his friendship circle." Lena spoke to friendship, New York intros, and, again, loyalty. She closed with, "I will think of you every time I dance, every time I eat bacon, every time I touch a waitress on the butt."

Natalie Kitroeff came next, then Eric Baker. Tim Carr followed, one of the other great speakers in our family. John Otis, longtime friend and fellow journalist, who flew in for the service from Colombia, recalled, "I think he took me to my first peep show."

One by one, mourners spoke to the different facets of his personality. The combinations seemed endless. How could one human be so many things? Still, one role had not been addressed: dad.

It is now or never. I had no notes. I walked up slowly to the pulpit, and then I heard myself talking. "I am going to be brief because I get to speak at the funeral tomorrow, but I did want to be sure to say that we—Jill, Madeline, Meagan, and I—are so thankful to all of you for being here." My voice seized, and I took a big gulp of air. I had no control over what came next; I wondered if I'd be able to make it through without sobbing uncontrollably.

"My dad was a crazy one," I started. "When we were born, a couple months premature, everyone thought it was not going to end well." I tried to express the pure and unquestioned faith he had in me and my professional abilities. I caught myself. *This is not about me; it is about him.*

"He told me I could do anything. And I want to say that to each and every one of you. You can do great things. I'm so sad he's not here, but goddamn, he would have loved this."

I exhaled and walked back to my seat. And then eight-year-old Lucy, the daughter of Erik Wemple and his wife, Stephanie Mencimer, hit the podium. "I don't want to make a speech, but David had a big personality and he never yelled at anyone." It was my favorite remark of the wake, because it was delivered by someone so young, so small, and so mighty. My dad would have been impressed.

His godson Chris Carr came next, and was followed by writer Seth Mnookin and wild boy Mike Carr. And then it was over.

While I had broken my nine-month sobriety a few months earlier, his death certainly fueled me with more ammunition to imbibe. We headed from the wake to a nearby bar, and countless people asked if I needed a drink. *Don't mind if I do.*

I had a nagging feeling that I should be somewhat sober for the funeral the next day, but my Irish heritage kicked in and I clocked out. I got blackout drunk for the fourth night in a row, one of the only things that made the feelings disappear.

They would reappear and grow like the Hydra overnight, but a couple of hours of numbness was all I needed.

My name is David Carr, and I'm an alcoholic. I think it's cool that
you guys have all these drunks and drug addicts and pirates up
here talking. . . .

Things have changed in a fundamental way. We talked a lot
about that. But just a quick note: My daughter Erin is a video
journalist. And I spent a lot of time trying to dissuade her from
getting involved in our business. She listened carefully, and went
the other way. You should do the same today.

My first story that I did was about police brutality. It was a
little local weekly, about thirty thousand people probably saw it.
Erin—same age, twenty-four years old—went and did a story
about a guy who used 3D printers to make guns to get around
federal gun laws, and I sort of head-patted her. I said, "That's a
cute project, that's a good idea, honey." Think it got twelve million hits on YouTube. I'd like to strangle her.

I'd like to strangle you guys, too, but I'm afraid I'll end up
working for you, so I'm going to suck up to you instead. . . .

I don't want to take an opportunity commencing at such an
august institution and not throwing down just short bits of advice.
I mean, you'd do it if you were up here, wouldn't you? Just a little
bit. These are ten bits of graduation advice you won't see on any
BuzzFeed listicle.

Remember my credentials, though. I was on welfare. I became
dependent on the state for both food and medical treatments. I
became a single parent at a time when no one would trust me
with a ficus plant. Other than that, I've been sort of a model citi-

zen. So take what applies and leave the rest, that's what I'm saying.

Right now, in your class, I know you guys are all having your kumbaya moment and you're hugging each other and saying how great you all are. But there are gunners, there are people who are really just heads and shoulders above everybody, and they're bound for glory. You know what? They're not the ones that are going to change the world. It's somebody that was underestimated. It's somebody that you do not know that's really going to kill it. I guarantee you. I guarantee you, as somebody who has worked with young people. And you know what? Maybe you're that person. I just want to say.

This has been a theme, and I just want to echo it, do what's in front of you. When you leave school, you've got your loans weighing down on you, you've got parents saying, "What the hell are you going to do with all this?" Just do what is in front of you. Don't worry about the plot to take over the world. Just do what is in front of you, and do it well. I think that if you concentrate on your plot to take over the world you're going to miss things.

Journalism is like housekeeping. It's a series of small, discrete acts performed over and over. It's really the little things that make it better. So don't think about the broad sweep of your journalism. Just do a good job on what's in front of you. Working on your grand plan is like shoveling snow that hasn't fallen yet. Just do the next right thing.

I think you should be a worker among workers. I say that because we're in an era of narcissism and personal brand. Don't worry about branding yourself, other than not being naked on your social feeds. I don't think it's really important for you to work a lot on brand development. I believe in social media engagement, and I've got a little problem with Twitter. It's more important that you fit in before you stick out, that's what I'm saying.

Number five is the mom rule. Don't do anything you couldn't explain to your ma. All these big, ethical conundrums where— [We] will run a three-day symposium on ethics, when in fact, if you can't explain what you're up to with your mother without her saying, "Honey, that seems a little naughty to me, what you're doing. It seems a little bad, that isn't nice." Don't do it. Don't go near it. Use the mom rule. Call her up. She's a great resource.

Don't just do what you're good at—that's number six. If you stay in your comfort zone, you'll never know what you're capable of. As has been pointed out, you need to learn to experience frustration, and you need to experience that frustration as a teachable moment, and you need to humble yourself and ask for help. Can you help me build my website? Yes, you can.

Being a journalist is permission for lifetime learning. Don't be a know-it-all. Ask the people around you.

Number seven is be present. I don't want to go all Oprah on you. So many people spend time like their phone right now is burning a hole in their pocket. Like, "Who's on there? What are they talking about?" And you know what's going on when you're thinking about that? Your whole life. Your whole life is going on.

I can't tell you the times I've gone to some extraordinary event or some conference where some big throbbing brain is talking. Everybody's walking around like this. They never look up. And it's like, if your head is in your phone, the scenery never changes. So don't worry about documenting the moment. Experience the moment.

I have close to half a million followers on Twitter, but the person who needs to know what I'm doing is me. Here I stand. This is what I'm doing. I got some pictures earlier, and I might tweet them out later, but Twitter isn't waiting to see what I think. I need to experience this extraordinary morning as it unfolds, and maybe later on I'll put a photo on Facebook or tweet something out.

Look at who you're speaking to. Get your face out of your phone. Do not be a bystander in your own life. You'll miss everything.

You should take responsibility for not just the good stuff, but the bad stuff. I have noticed in leadership, in covering people over and over, it's the people who are capable of taking ownership over failure, and apologizing very directly for their shortcomings, that succeed.

We're all broken, in one way or another. To pretend or expect otherwise is stupid. And when you come up short, just say so, don't make excuses. Excuses—they explain everything and they excuse nothing. Just be honest about what you did wrong, take ownership, and resolve to do better.

I think it's very important, this number nine, is to be honest. This is a tactical approach these days. People always say, "I love that thing you've got where you just say whatever's on your mind. You just come right out with it. It's, like, you know, the truth." It's, like, well, that's not really a tactic. That's a way of living. That's a way of being.

When you're honest with someone, when the door opens and you have to have a difficult conversation, just walk through it and have the difficult conversation. Show the people in front of you the respect to be honest with them.

One of the things I hate about being in California is you guys always, when you talk, you sound like you're agreeing with each other. You're not! You're having—"Oh I totally hear what you're saying and I'm sure we can work with that. We obviously gotta loop in some other"—and it's like, "No, you're wrong, I'm right, here's why."

When you develop this gimmick, this reputation for telling the truth, people tend to listen to what you say.

And last thing is don't be afraid to be ambitious. I'm living a pipe dream, and I'm living it because I wanted it. I wanted it really badly. I was thirty-four years old, washed out of my profession, on welfare, terrible reputation, single parent, and I had just met the woman who would be my wife. And she said, "Where do you see yourself five years from now?" I said, "Well, I want to be a figure on the national media scene." And she said, "Well, honey, you're unemployed and you're on welfare right now, so, there's like a middle part." "I know! I'm just trying to articulate a goal."

The other thing I'd say is the people who doubt you, like you're gonna get out of here and you're gonna have friends who got their MBA who are working for Morgan Stanley or whoever they're working for, they're working for a hot dot-com. And they say, "Well, good luck with that, you're going to sink below the waist." Those are your friends, the people who doubt you. Because you're going to make fools out of them.

I often think of the people who never thought I would do anything. Those are your allies. Those are your little secret friends. You keep them close.

I think that what's important— I was on a panel with Gay Talese, the great *New York Times* journalist, great narrative journalist. And people were asking him about the current age of journalism, where, you know, we're Boswells. We sit in a cube and we write about people who write about people who write about—that we end up in this meta, crazy place where we don't have anything original, we're just putting a little topspin on whatever's going by.

And the great Gay Talese said, "We are outside people. We leave, we find people more interesting than us, and we come back and we tell their stories."

Right now, everything looks impossible. Think back when you applied to be here. How many bodies did you crawl over to get here, for one thing? You're extraordinary just by getting in here. And now you made it to the end—improbably, not everyone probably did, but *you're* here. *You're* standing here. So when you see the big incline ahead of you, just keep in mind these last two years. You totally beat the odds, and you fucking landed it. You're here!

Odds against you, here you stand. Grads of the Berkeley School of Journalism. Resolve to be worthy of that. Resolve to do important things with that. Be grateful for the good things that have come your way.

This small group before you, ladies and gentlemen, will I'm sure one day make a big dent in this world. Maybe somebody should write a story about that.

My deepest congratulations to you, the family; you, the faculty; but most of all, you guys. I'm proud of ya and I don't even know ya.

26

His Second Act

"Still alive."

As I woke up I was hit with the undeniable fact that today was my father's funeral. I tried to will my eyes to open, but they were swollen and crusted together from all of the past days' crying. I was in bed in the attic of our family home in New Jersey. I cringed as I began to conjure the things I did or said the night before. I'd held it together at the wake but then all went to hell as I drowned in white wine and grief. I dimly recalled begging my twin to sleep next to me, but when I awoke the place in the bed where her body was supposed to be was vacant. I turned over and faced the light and there she was, quietly folding a sweater into her suitcase. She didn't look up but said good morning all the same. The air up in the attic smelled still, unfamiliar. I couldn't remember how I got up there.

I asked her if everything was okay.

"Not really."

"Will you help me get ready?"

"Sure."

I got out of bed and reached for the water next to the nightstand that she had most likely put there. "I don't want to talk about last night," I started. "Later, we can discuss it, just not right now."

She remained silent. I hugged her and she hugged me back, but there was reluctance in her embrace.

We headed down into my bedroom—the room I was supposed to sleep in but refused to in a drunken stupor—and I kicked open the suitcase on the floor. Yunna and her mom had gone out and bought some black dresses for me to try on. There was a liquid-like leather dress that my contrarian side wanted to pick, knowing that Dad would hate it. But Meagan chose the simple black cotton one for me. I showered quickly and blow-dried my hair and put my glasses on, a good shield for the tears that would be forthcoming. My face was bloated, having aged remarkably over the previous week.

A hangover was descending quickly. I knew I should be sober for what was coming next but I wouldn't be. I couldn't be. We three would be speaking in front of seven hundred or so people.

The hangover continued to blur everything until I was outside St. Ignatius Loyola church on Park Avenue. It was bitterly cold (much like the night he died), and there was a lone bagpiper belting out the Irish melodies of yesteryear. My stepmom had hired him, giving my father a proper Irish goodbye. I fumbled around in my black blazer pocket for the Adderall I had pocketed from my roommate's stash. I'd since kicked him out, but had a couple of remaining pills left for very special occasions. This felt like one of those moments. I didn't feel good about stealing it, but there was this weird thought that kept circling my brain: *I deserve this.* It was a lie; I deserved nothing.

The bagpiper motioned for my stepmom to come over. The church wouldn't allow him inside and with the wind chill, it was below freezing. He couldn't feel his fingers. Jill nodded and told him she understood. He put his hands inside his cloak, grateful for the reprieve. I left them and headed into the church. I heard my heels click on the lavish marble that lined the inside of the church hall. I marveled at my surroundings. Even in death, he had arrived.

Stained-glass windows lined the hall, and I noticed that if you stared long enough into one of them, you could forget why you were there. Momentarily.

The funeral felt different from the wake. People were somber and quiet, saying only the bare minimum. I noticed how attractive my boyfriend looked in his suit. We held hands and stared straight ahead toward the altar. The room filled to the brim with people, and I was once again impressed by the gravitational pull of my late departed dad. I wondered where he was sitting for this encore presentation.

The service began and continued without disruption, and I was riveted by the stories once again. My sisters and I got up to speak. Meagan was first, her tone cautious, slow, deliberate.

My dad used to always say that everything good in his life started with us. But the truth is so many of the good things that happened in our lives and the lives of many of the people here today started with my dad. He was a devoted husband and father, unflagging mentor, and a dear friend. In my lifetime, I will likely never know a person who touched as many people as my dad did. And despite the abundance of attention and accolades, which is highly deserved, what I will remember most about my dad is so much simpler and quieter.

When my dad and I were together, we talked about cooking, Jill, Erin, Maddie, Ed. We talked about projects around the house and sometimes work. This is not to say we had a facile relationship, only that we had just as much fun talking about those things as we did talking about the important topics.

And yet, my dad's counsel on important matters was irreplaceable. This is the one thing I will remember most, and I wanted to end today by sharing some of the things I learned from my dad with each of you. Mean what you say. This is a flagship value in our family, and it is integral to living with integrity. Down to every last swear word, my dad was genuine about what he said and he taught us to do the same. Do something you love and work hard. This is a characteristic that so many of you are familiar with but as someone who bore witness to it almost every day of my twenty-six years, it was indeed breathtaking. My dad was, yes, of course, driven and ambitious, but he was devoted, too. He cared so much about what he did, and I know his passion inspired others. Always, always say I love you, or as my dad would say to me, almost every time we spoke, "I adore you." In good times and in bad, my father told me unfailingly that he loved me, cared for me, respected me. In my relationships, I aspire to be half as loving and compassionate as he was.

She wiped away some tears and left the podium.

Madeline stepped up. She spoke fast, willing herself to get through it.

My dad had a bit of a hang-up on memory, on its nature, its purpose, and the natural inclination to modify the past to accommodate the ones we love, most often ourselves. In the wake of his death, I found myself scrambling to remember all the times we spent together—the good, the bad, the ugly— with the hope of securing at least the smallest thing to hold on to. As my father's daughter, I question the authenticity of the recollection: How much of this am I fabricating? Glorifying? Enhancing?

And then I see all of you. The most honest testament to the man he was. Each and every one of you has your own piece of David Carr to confirm my shaky memories. We are here to celebrate a man who touched so many lives in so many ways. I wasn't super-close with David Carr the professional, or David Carr the young man, but I discovered that those people weren't so different from my David Carr, the family man.

Regardless of which of the hats my dad was wearing, he could be counted on for advice, whether you knew you needed it or not. I treasure his wisdom but I can't seem to apply it to this new and scary territory. He frequently urged me to stop trying to wrap my head around things and to instead wrap my arms around them. But you know, what I certainly cannot wrap my head around is his absence, and I dearly want to wrap my arms around him.

It was my turn. I started by echoing the sentiment that started my twin's eulogy. There is a video of this moment. I steel myself in the present day to watch it but need to turn away the second I appear onscreen. My face is swollen, the dress is too tight, and the words that I so carefully chose become garbled in my mouth. I remember wanting to channel him, in this singular moment, his irreverent style. I wanted to say something unique about someone I loved so dearly. But my brain was foggy due to grief and substances and so, instead, I started by mumbling, the moment too big for me to bear.

I think you may have heard this but it deserves repeating.
"Everything good started with you" is what my father would say to my twin sister, Meagan, and I. But the truth was it was the other way around. My dad represented a blinding and fierce force in my life that will not be forgotten. When we

were little kids my dad would take us for a ride when he had
something important to tell us.

I again stumbled over the words but continued.

One time he looked at us from the rearview mirror and
asked us how we would feel about him asking Jilly to marry
him. "What about a ring?" Meagan asked. Girls, we always
know how to talk about jewels. Marry they did. My dad
loved Jill within an inch of her life, and a short number of
years later they had Madeline, our darling and ever serious
little sister.
   Our lives are full of magic, and that's what I want to talk
about. My parents had a wood-paneled and rustic cabin in
the Adirondack mountain range; it was his good friend Erik
Wemple's cabin before it was ours. My dad and I so loved that
cabin. Dad loved to build these giant fires, and when I say
large I mean nine feet and sometimes lit with diesel fuel.

There was a huge laugh and I felt buoyed. I was doing what he
would have done.

That's the kind of guy my dad is. Do the big, that's always how
it went. Jill would put Celine Dion on the crappy stereo and
my dad and his girls would trundle down to the community
house to play ping-pong after. My dad would always win and
would always let us know.
   I work in the media world—lord knows this gal wanted to
follow in her dad's footsteps. He legitimately did a talk the
night he passed. I went backstage, eager to meet the people he
spoke to. When I shook Glenn's hand, he said, "Your dad
never shuts up about you! He came to Rio and all he wanted

to talk about was you. He is your biggest fan." I stated matter-
of-factly, "And I am his."

My dad, as all you know, was a brilliant mind and com-
passionate human. He was a curious sort and wanted to
know about everything. I honor him by attempting to do the
same.

When we were little, my dad would have us say, "Make
way for El Rey" when we opened up the door. Well, today,
make way for El Rey now.

I'm not sure if I made El Rey, aka the king, proud with my
words. But I had gotten through it, and that was a feat in and of
itself. I moved toward my pew and sat down, removing my
glasses and crying as silently as possible. Meagan grabbed my
hand and squeezed it.

Near the end of the service, a *Times* photographer began
clicking his camera. I didn't understand why he was there. Why
would this be an important moment to capture for the paper?
Hadn't there been enough of that? The final prayer was said out
loud, and I was instructed to head to the back of the church for
the receiving line of condolences.

I said little when people came up to me, but I did hug. Words
were escaping me. David Remnick, editor of *The New Yorker*,
made his way up to me. I was surprised; I'd only met him a
couple of times during the outings he and my dad took to the
U.S. Open every year. I'd sent him a couple of links of my work
at the request of my dad, but I didn't know him well at all. I
braced myself.

David's face was warm and expressive as his dark eyes looked
down at me. "F. Scott Fitzgerald said that there are no second
acts in life. Your father proved that smart man wrong. What a
hell of a second act." He moved along quickly, but made sure to

mention that he'd stay in touch. I nodded and mentally made a note, as my dad would have had me do.

The bagpiper had warmed up enough to play as the mass of people exited the church to head down to the basement for cheese and tepid white wine. Another photo was snapped for the *Times*. Days later I carefully studied it. In the photo I am following Jill and Madeline down the stone steps. I'm either smiling or grimacing, my mouth open, perhaps saying something. I couldn't tell. Once again, my memory was a blur. But the photo served as documentation that at least this part was over.

27

Traces

"Writing is choosing."

Sudden death creates a creeping sensation that you are living in an alternate reality. In the days after the funeral, when I returned to the house, I would look through his bedroom door. His room remained the same, despite the fact that he would never return to it. The soft light blue sweater was hung over the upholstered white chair. Thick nonfiction books and ballpoint pens lined the nightstand, books he set out to read but now wouldn't. The black VAIO laptop remained plugged in, awaiting his return.

Charlie, our middle-aged white lab, sat patiently in the kitchen staring at the back door, lifting her head up ever so slightly to try to see through the fogged glass. Is that him? Is he coming? I whispered to her that I loved her just as much as he did. I hugged her the way he would, a giant embrace. We were sisters.

She died two weeks after him; I understand how she must have felt.

Objects tell us the stories of the people who held them. I see this at the cabin and our house. What they valued and cherished and what they couldn't live without. It's hundreds of things that are each a self-contained puzzle piece. In the weeks after his death, Jill told us to start thinking about what things of his we might want. But he didn't care much for stuff. Give him a headset, a notebook, and a comfy cashmere sweater and he was set. I didn't feel the same way. I wanted *him*. I was looking for something.

Madeline had made sure to grab a couple of the flowers from the funeral. Perfect long-stemmed white roses. It was decided that we wanted to save these perennial artifacts and encase them in a clear resin. I was not sure if I wanted a memento to remember one of the worst days of our lives.

We set out for the hobby store Michaels in our parkas. The winter was unrelenting. My eyes took in the scene of mostly women wandering the aisles, some with their kids, and I was hit with a wave of normalcy. People were out living their lives even though it felt like ours was ending. The fluorescent lights made my skull reverberate. I started to grow queasy. I wanted to get out of there as soon as humanly possible.

When I asked Meagan and Madeline how long they expected we'd be, they put me to work and tasked me with finding a glass receptacle for the dead dad flowers. I skulked off in search of the right aisle. Meagan called after me, but I didn't turn around. My wet boots squeaked on the linoleum floor as I got to the glass department of the godforsaken craft store. I stood there and considered scooping up all the containers and sending them crashing to the ground. I was electrified by the thought of destruction. I craved the feeling. I got close and grabbed a cheap plastic vase, but it wouldn't have had the satisfying smash I wanted it to. I placed it back on the shelf and recognized what I was doing. I grabbed three glass jars, thick ones, and put them in a basket. I walked away from my fantasy and back toward the nightmare.

When we got home Jill told us we had to do our arts and crafts project in the basement because the resin could get everywhere. As my sisters spread out their craft loot, I stood back, hoping to offer moral support rather than creative contributions. "I'll just get in the way," I said. Meagan rolled her eyes and Madeline followed suit.

The canister of resin was unlocked, and noxious fumes filled the air. Madeline wore gloves as she carefully poured the liquid gel into the container holding one white rose. The rose faltered and started to tip to the right side, the gel unevenly filling up the small round jar. It was the first pancake of the bunch and I claimed it as mine. I like things a little off-center.

We left the roses to set and I headed upstairs and looked at his desk in the dining room. It wasn't really a desk, just a repository for things he was supposed to look at next. He preferred to be mobile, drifting from one room to the next with his laptop in hand. I picked up his leather wallet with his driver's license. He was carrying it in his pocket when he collapsed. I opened it, feeling cautious, as if he might yell at me. In the ID photo he was unsmiling but looking darn handsome. His *New York Times* business cards were stuffed in little slits, and there was cash in the billfold. I brought it up to my face and smelled it. The leather mixed with the stale tobacco and I was taken back to his presence, to that last hug outside on the sidewalk. I closed my eyes and allowed myself to feel it.

I was startled when Meagan walked in on me, her hands still in gloves. I stammered nervously. "Oh, ya know, just smelling his belongings."

She stifled a chortle. "I get it."

She left the room, and I placed the wallet on the desk exactly where I'd found it. I saw a series of reporter's notebooks, filled to the brim with his trademark scrawls. I grabbed one and took it upstairs to my childhood bedroom and sat down on the edge of the quilt-covered bed.

This room, my room, felt empty now. The notebook housed

clues, but I couldn't make complete sense of it. Just one mystery after another as my brain fogged with gut-rotting sadness.

As weeks passed I couldn't help but text him. Because we'd been so digitally tethered, it felt only normal, albeit a bit morbid.

One night I wrote, "I'm sorry I didn't act more grateful when you gave me that sweater at Christmas." The message felt like the panicked act of a kid who has forgotten her algebra assignment. I wanted him to know that I was appreciative and that I loved that he got me a sweater that reminded me of his own sweaters.

I sometimes feel like an inferior version of his doppelgänger. I have his DNA, but am not him. Our text history is short. I deleted a majority of them to free up space on my phone and I curse myself for it. But I still have his emails. I typed in C A R R 2 N @ G M A I L . C O M again and clicked through page after page of our back-and-forth.

I created a Google document and start copying and pasting my favorite lines:

"Find myself thinking about you a lot. Wondering what kind of adventures you're living, learning you are doing, tasks you are on."

"i'd be working every angle."

When I closed my eyes I could hear him saying those things out loud. Whenever I would send him a flare email, his response was always relentlessly positive and made me feel like I was part of a tribe, a team. That someone was taking care of me. I knew, then and now, that this was a rare relationship for a child to have with a parent.

For the most part, parents love and want to protect their children, but how many of us really know one another? I wondered what caused this sense of closeness, and I realized I'd never even asked him this. My educated guess was that there was some guilt about our unseemly origin story involving cocaine and later crack. We were premature babies born to our mother while the two of them battled their demons. My mother fled back into her disease while my dad sought treatment. He wanted to ensure that nothing like that ever happened again. That his story would protect our own; we would be the successful women he knew us to be.

The words were there, archived. But he was not an active part of the conversation anymore. I had so many questions for him. How on earth could I find the answers?

How do I have a career without you?
What else did you want to do?
Was my moderate success because of you?
How do I live sober?
How can we remain a family without you?
Why were you so hard on me?
Why were you so hard on yourself?
Did part of you know you were going to die?
What do you wish you had told me before you died?

The information exists within his digital sphere. I move toward the emails, the Gchats, texts, and tweets. Data for me to mine. Possible answers to my many, many questions.

28

The Upside of Getting Fired

"My, you just keep turning out. You are full of surprises."

My first HBO film, *Thought Crimes,* premiered at the Tribeca Film Festival in April 2015. Any novice filmmaker would be nervous, but I also felt tremendous gratitude. I had finished something I set out to do, a feat I was unsure I was capable of after my firing. And I had reason other than delusion to be confident about the film.

Five months before, I had screened the movie for my family. The perfect ending to a nice Thanksgiving meal. With our bellies full of turkey and stuffing we headed upstairs to Dad and Jill's bedroom to see what these blood relatives of mine had to say about the documentary I had made. The room, decorated many moons ago, always made me feel comfortable. The walls and comforter were a deep textured green; a Picasso print hung above their California king bed. A coin dish sat on the bureau, filled to the brim with AA coins, pens, and a shamrock bowtie. I asked if I could use a pen.

I was excited to get my dad's feedback—his opinion was one of the few I trusted completely and without question. The room was mostly silent as Meagan, Jill, Madeline, my dad, and I made our way through the film with a couple of laughs and groans. I sat on the floor as I didn't want to be the weirdo that watches her family during screenings.

As the credits rolled, helped along by KISS's "New York Groove," I stayed silent. Dad was the first to speak. "Well, you fucking did it. Smashing job." The rest of the family exalted the film with praise, and each member took turns dissecting parts they loved or were confused by. My dad did have one big criticism: We show the supposed Cannibal Cop eating *wayyyyy* too much. He called it a "skull fuck." Did I mention he cursed a lot?

My dad and I had been plotting for months on who to invite to the premiere. I had been, let's just say, an out-of-work loser for a little bit, and he was grateful to shift gears and have a second kid he could brag about (my ever-achieving twin sister had just started her PhD program). Now that was a wash. I invited the people on our list, but felt super self-conscious, like a junior high nerd sending out Evites to a basement party that people wouldn't want to go to.

Very true to my modest Midwestern roots, I rented a dress for the occasion. A brilliant blue dress made by Monique Lhuillier, it was bejeweled at the waist, with pockets to tuck my hands in. I looked the part, but now I had to act it.

My sisters and I took a car service over to the venue. I was pretty much silent the whole ride, anxious about the speech I had to make. Meagan asked me not to drink, and I begrudgingly promised her I wouldn't.

I stepped out of the car in my much-too-high nude pumps from DSW. I regained my composure and was invited to walk my first-ever red carpet for a film I had made. I smiled slyly, making sure not to show any of my slightly crooked teeth. I felt beautiful and cool. Jill came up to me, done up nicely, and asked for my palm. In it she placed a small metal Buddha figurine and squeezed my hand closed around it. Before I could say anything, she said, "Dad would be so proud," and strode away as quickly as she had come. He had died two months prior, but he would have no doubt wanted the show to go on.

It was time to give the introduction, and I pulled it off without a hitch, making sure to mention Gil's courage in participating but also my dad's guidance. I spoke plainly and earnestly into the microphone: "To my father, who taught me truth is a hard-won battle but to strive for it at all costs." I knew instinctively to mention the living: "To all the women in my little Carr family who are inspirations and give me the strength to carry on." And with that I sat in the front row and the iconic HBO static reverberated in my head and on the screen. I had done it.

A smile crept onto my face and I felt a rush of gratitude for an opportunity that few are afforded. My dad had told me that being unceremoniously fired would be one of the best things that ever happened to me; he was right. It made room in my life for this. He was always right. Throughout the night, I felt a push and pull of grief and happiness. I was on a panel with Alan Dershowitz, drinking a Shirley Temple with one of my favorite filmmakers, Alex Gibney, and dancing on the bed at the Standard hotel, toasting my dear friends for all the help they had given me. How could he have missed this?

29

Chatter

When your parent, child, close relative, or partner dies, you get a pass to eat whatever you want. In my case it was buckets of Velveeta Shells and Cheese, the kind my dad used to make when we were kids, white trash by way of the Midwest. The pass also gets you out of work when you can't hang in anymore, the excuse to cancel on anyone at any time, and, oh yeah, to drink whatever you want. You have real pain. The only way through it is to medicate, right?

After sitting by myself for all of twenty minutes in my apartment I would become twitchy. One night I texted my friend Kathleen and begged her to meet me. We went to a nearby bar where she bought me drinks, even though I knew she didn't really have the scratch to spare. The feeling of being pitied—I hate that I like it.

I drank eight glasses of cheap white wine over the course of many hours. When we got back to the apartment, I pulled *The Night of the Gun* off the bookshelf and drunkenly read it out loud. I knew I was making my friend super uncomfortable, but she placated me by listening. What a nightmare. My roommate Yunna was awakened by the commotion and came out and stared at me through bleary eyes. She quietly asked if we could keep it down. I cried and told her I would try. When Kathleen left I continued drinking and reading my father's book. I could hear him.

It had been two months since my dad died, and while I was spiritually thin, I was otherwise large, the continuous cycle of wine and pasta quickly leading to a fifteen-pound weight gain. *Anything to stop the feelings,* I muttered inside my own head. After another boozy night, I had to decide whether I was going to get up and face the day or spend it in bed. No one would care either way. I decided to text my twin.

Me: Waking up is the worst

MMC: Tell me about it

Me: How many times have you cried today?

MMC: 5

Me: But it's not even 10am.

MMC: I know.

I often asked my dad the question "How do you do the next right thing?" He responded, "you wake up and things are better. that's how." But things do not seem better upon waking; they feel the same. Limbo.

I headed toward the bathroom, praying that my roommates weren't home. I didn't want to be accountable to anyone. I walked past the front door and glanced at my dad's obituary taped to the back of it. Yunna had taped it there, just like we did at our house in Montclair. "David Carr, *Times* Critic and Champion of Media, Dies at 58." It's my dad's face in a black-and-white photo, his chin propped up in his hand. He looks youthful, charming, curious. It was a picture I had never seen before. I stared at it. I wondered if it was healthy to have this exposed, so readily available. But the alternative—taking it down—seemed like sacrilege. I went to the bathroom and looked at myself in the mirror. I looked like shit. But again, I kind of liked it. My outsides matched my insides.

But I couldn't stay there all day. I raced to get to the bus on time at the Port Authority. Jill had asked us to come back to Montclair for a family dinner. The sweat was dripping down my face despite the brisk air. I was hungover from the night before, and there was a deep pulse in my head that kept vibrating every thirty seconds or so. I checked my phone and the glow hurt my eyes. I closed them while I waited at the terminal. The sheer number of drug addicts and New York commuters tend to make for a combustible atmosphere at the Port Authority.

It was 4:56 when I got on the bus. I remembered that my headphones weren't working. This was like the fifth set in a row that I'd broken. I was forced to be alone with my thoughts. I stared out the dirty window of DeCamp 66, the bus I would take home to see him. "Hello, Dolly," he'd say. "How was the trip out?" I was on the bus fantasizing about having that moment again. My ears pricked up when I heard my dad's name. I wondered if I was having a hallucination.

"Yeah, David Carr, he rode this bus all the time. He actually died at the *New York Times* building." I felt like I could hear her shuddering. I glanced behind me to see who was speaking. She was a nondescript woman in her mid-fifties with brown hair. I guessed my family had now become a sort of urban legend. A bit of news for someone to talk about on their ride home from work. I considered shouting at her: *"Maybe you shouldn't say things like that when his kid is sitting next to you on this bus."* But instead, I kept my mouth shut.

The woman got off at her stop, and I did the same a few minutes later. I felt anxious as I exited but I made sure to mumble a thank-you to the driver. My headache would not relent and I wondered how useful that bottle of white wine the night before

really was. I thought about the house. For my sisters, it represented a place of goodness and memories. To me? It was full of
ghosts. I walked to the back porch and found it locked. I
searched for the key in the cupboard on the porch. Nothing. I
called Madeline, who was upstairs. I heard her tumble toward
the door and felt irrationally full of rage. Why do I have to call
to be let in?

We were sitting at dinner later when I asked my stepmom
about the key situation. "The key was missing from the cupboard," I said softly.

Jill put down her silverware and stared at me. "I am a woman
who lives alone. I can't have keys left out anymore."

From a rational point of view, I knew she was right. She was
undergoing this seismic change, and it was her house, not mine.
I heard her continue on about the possibility of being assaulted
while she was alone at night, but I closed my eyes, unsure of
what to say next. "Okay, well, is it possible to get a key to use
when I come home then?"

She looked down but stated clearly, "I don't think so." She
said something about too many sets of keys being available for
the house. My head started buzzing and I realized this was how
it happens, this was how you get locked out of your own family
home. I thought about starting an altercation, screaming at her
that her child—my baby sister, Madeline—had a set of keys, so
why should it be any different for her other daughters? Me and
my twin. Just like on the bus, I kept my mouth shut.

That's how families break apart after a death. Quiet, startling
moments that define how you treat one another. I am my father's daughter. I have a mother and a stepmom.

Meagan talked to Madeline and they made a secret plan to
make house key copies to fix the problem. My baby sister
handed me a silver key on a green ring to add to my keychain. I
never got around to using it.

30

The Castle Without Its El Rey

"Times like this, it's great to belong to a family like ours."

Eventually, Jill asked us to come to New Jersey and clean out the house. It was time to sell. A five-bedroom colonial no longer made sense for a widow. I often wondered what Jill was doing at any given moment after my dad's death. What was it like to wake up with someone for twenty years and then have them gone, almost as if they'd evaporated? I don't ask her about these things. We're not close enough for me to pose such an intimate question.

I dreaded every day leading up to that weekend. I tried to distract myself with work, but even there, tension was rising. I worked with a small team of dedicated and smart people with Andrew as our leader. The week before the move he gently asked how I was doing. "Terrible, the thought of it makes me want to gouge my eyeballs out." I didn't know what else to say. I knew many people had moved belongings out of their deceased parents' houses. I was not a special snowflake and *yet*. The pain felt unique as ever.

I drove out there on a Sunday morning, a gnawing pain surfacing every few minutes in the pit of my stomach. It was one of those beautiful sunny days that seem to make a mockery of your grief. The whole world keeps moving and whirling while you stand still, unable to enjoy anything for even a minute. I was frightened at the prospect of doing something so final, taking away the last remaining pieces of the puzzle, dismantling the family we used to be.

Once we all arrived, it was smiles throughout. The Carr girls put on their battle faces, but in that Minnesota way that necessitates good cheer.

We started in the garage, a place of little sentimentality. Eight rakes, myriad sets of gloves, and the occasional "hoe" joke, and we were off to the races. The trash bags started piling up and sweat dripped from my forehead.

"Hey, this isn't so bad," I said to my twin.

She grimaced and softly said, "Well, good, but we haven't gotten to the rough stuff."

I peered into my former bedroom. All of my stuff from childhood was gone. My dad had politely requested that I remove my detritus when I hit twenty-five, saying he wanted the room back. I felt betrayed, but I complied. Afterward Jill lined my room with garment racks, and my twin's room was filled with workout gear. Maddie was allowed to keep hers as is. Salt in the wound.

I soon realized that it was not my house. I was fortunate enough to have an office *and* a cramped apartment in Queens in which to store my memorabilia. It dawned on me that this was their home and they got to do whatever they saw fit in those rooms.

Meagan's bedroom eventually became less of a repository for weights and more of a personal shrine. He'd placed a small desk, a chest of wooden drawers with a mirror attached, and a crappy Ikea couch that I knew he hated in there. But the walls were what made the room the room. Throughout his career, my dad had garnered hundreds of press badges: CNN, HBO, SXSW, Sundance, the Oscars, all with his smileless mug and the ever-important *Times* credential on a piece of laminated plastic.

Maddie—whom my dad liked to call Matthew, as she was the most technically skilled among us and because we think he wanted, just a little bit, a son—had taken it upon herself to tape all the badges together. My dad hung her creation up over his desk, in a tribute to all the places he had gone and seen. The badges dislodged and the collage fell apart after he died.

There was a giant French poster of *Page One: Inside the New York Times* on the north wall, with the best picture of my dad in a Santa hat in front of it. Framed photos lined the wall with, oh yeah, his face. The *Times* had published a full-page ad of my dad with the headline FIND OUT WHAT OUR REPORTERS ARE READING. He is almost smiling in this picture, almost. Lena Dunham had sent him an illustration of him sitting at a *Girls* party, neck bent low, very thoughtful. He'd hung it on the wall with a sense of pride. When I first saw what was formerly my sister's room, I have to be honest: I was pretty creeped out. Who makes a shrine to themselves? This felt borderline narcissistic.

But after he died, it was one of the few things that made complete sense. This was dad's room, his memorial. This was exactly the right place where we could keep all of his stuff. Each of us could walk into the room and feel close to him. But now, it was time to dismantle it.

I spent most of the day mired in self-pity. I was packing up my remaining childhood effects, which had been left in the basement, marveling at how many collages of *Dawson's Creek* one young girl could make. "Whatcha doing in here?" Meagan asked me.

I had not been good about spending time with the family as of late. I felt edgy and wanted to be left alone. I looked up and for the first time in a long time was able to see outside of myself. It occurred to me how hard this part must have been for her, my twin. The family home was not something I cared much about, but for Meagan it was a very intense source of comfort. My dad would always be the first to volunteer to pick her up from the airport while at the same time making sure something was bubbling in the Crock-Pot to welcome her home. To him, cooking meant love. It was a form of service.

Now, no one offered to pick her up. She had to ask. Meagan was empathetic to a fault. Blond, fit, and friendly, she could have been mistaken for someone who had it all figured out. I didn't think she did, and I mean that in a good way. She was continually searching and probing the world for answers. Her PhD program was grueling, and she was underpaid. She complained only when shit really sucked, which it did often. Underneath the smile I knew she was struggling. Her depression was fully active and she was still not sleeping all these months later. She told me that she couldn't manage to eat much, that she'd made peanut butter and jelly sandwiches for dinner many nights in a row, unable to put in the effort to make anything else.

We sat together in the shrine room, taking it in. I thought about asking her to hold me, but I realized it wasn't one of those moments. She wanted to be left alone in her grief. Even together, we were alone.

Jill started to lay my dad's clothes on the bed. Well-worn sweaters, stained white dress shirts. Then came the real magic: his T-shirts. Rock 'n' roll, BBQ, and writing were common themes in his collection. My favorites included a WILL WRITE FOR FOOD shirt I made him, and a tee with an upside-down NEW YORK. I grabbed a bike shirt he wore constantly during his time on the trails, and the three of us lobbied for the remaining belongings. This was where things might get heated in other families but not in ours. Belongings did not make up our dad; it was just stuff.

I walked away with a *New York Times* hat, one of his favorite cashmere sweaters, and an armful of T-shirts. I knew I wouldn't wear most of the stuff. But I would keep it safe.

31

If It's Not Getting Better,
Consider the Alternative

In the months after my dad died I knew that my alcoholism was becoming worse, but I was unable to envision a future that did not include substances in some way. My dad was dead, and so I drank wine. A lot of it. That said, I knew that there had to be some safeguards in check, so I wouldn't go completely off the rails. I developed a plan and wrote it down in my notebook. I would attempt some degree of sobriety, on occasion.

With this new plan in place, I knew I had a couple of challenges to get through over the next few weeks. My college friend Anna was coming to stay, and I desperately wanted to show her a good time. I had emailed her beforehand with a delightful bingo game of New York sights/events that we could take part in. I also told her that I would not be drinking. She had no problem with us not drinking, she wrote back; in fact, she preferred it. The second I saw that in the email, my stomach plummeted. I really didn't want to go to a burlesque performance and order a seltzer. I wanted tequila, some delish champagne, or a gin and tonic, goddammit.

An avid talker and listener, Anna comes from good Wisconsin stock. She has neat brown hair, cut at her shoulders, and has a penchant for Bob Dylan. I always think of her with an apple in her right hand. She is a real sweetheart, and the last time she'd visited me I'd been a drunken mess. I promised myself it was not going to be the same this time.

We cackled like crones when she arrived at my newly tidied Brooklyn apartment. Yunna welcomed her and we drank coffee with creamer and had scones that I had picked up from the local bakery up the street, like a good adult hostess. I was going to get through this weekend with grace and dignity.

We headed to the Whitney and saw some new exhibits and then ventured to a Spanish restaurant for some tapas. My eyes glanced at the red wine available on the menu and my mouth watered. I found myself ordering a Diet Coke, and Anna was fine with water. Suddenly the bacon-wrapped date that came to the table tasted subpar. I just wanted some wine. And to then relax into the conversation with this lovely woman I hadn't seen in years. I craved the easy intimacy that came with alcohol.

After dinner we headed to the Strand to peruse the miles of adventures and the books that held them. We separated among the stacks and I started to plot about how to pitch her on the idea of drinking. I practiced the words, all the while completely understanding that this was *not* normal behavior. On the L train back to my borough, I lied to her that my alcohol issues had been getting better, but that abstinence would not be a workable solution for me. I volunteered to pay for some fancy rosé to help us pregame before our glittering night at the Slipper Room, a notorious playground/burlesque club on the Lower East Side. She looked disappointed, but knew from years of experience that if I was going to drink, no one was going to stop me.

The second my hands gripped the glass bottle out of the chic winery's mini refrigerator, I felt, in a strange way, calmer: I was going to have access to the medicine I needed. I bought two bottles of wine plus a case of Modelo beer, justifying the purchase by saying we had a couple of nights together and we would want to be stocked. I knew I would be drinking one of those bottles by myself, and I didn't want to share.

The visit I had so carefully planned turned into an excuse for me to get as drunk as possible, as quickly as possible. Oh, and the meaningful conversation I sought at the tapas restaurant, the fact that I thought booze was the way to unlock some sort of intimacy, was a complete joke. I basically ended up ignoring this woman who had flown nearly a thousand miles to be near me.

After the show, back at the apartment and sufficiently buzzed, I ordered some cocaine. She wanted no part of it. I picked up my laptop and moved into the living room to type until late hours of the night, about absolutely nothing.

I woke up the next morning asleep on the couch, fully dressed, black eyeliner dripping off the sides of my face. I was *so fucking hungover.* I could barely take a breath without it hurting my head. But wait, we had lunch planned with Jasper at eleven. I groaned as I realized it was ten now. I didn't want him to think anything was amiss, so I would have to rally and rally hard. I knew what might help. Gingerly, I crept over to the refrigerator and saw the untouched beer glinting at me. Trying to be as quiet as possible, I grabbed two out of the cardboard box and ran into the bathroom and turned the metal lock on the door to the right. I turned on the shower to disguise the sound of the beer opening. I nervously thought that either Yunna or Anna might hear, but I couldn't worry about that. I opened the first one and sat on the lid of the toilet.

Oh my God, this is why people do this. It felt so nice and reassuring to introduce the alcohol back into my nervous system. I drank the beer in one sitting and stood up to look at myself in the mirror. I knew what had just happened was the next stage of a progressive disease. I was now drinking in the morning and hiding it. My blue eyes stared back at me. It wasn't so unforgivable, was it? I brought the second beer with me into the shower and drank it while the scalding water beat down at my back. It was so soothing and I felt the internal warmth coming back to me; it was going to be *okaaaaay.*

I hopped out of the shower and stashed the beer cans in the wooden cabinet behind a giant box of tampons. I walked into my room, and Anna was sitting up and reading a book. She looked irritated, but I wasn't about to get into it. I informed her that we would take a cab to Astoria, and Jasper would then drive us to an amazing, locals-only dim sum shop. I could tell that she was surprised that I was rallying, but she didn't remark on it.

My buzz started to wear off the second we got to the dumpling shack. There was no way for me to order a beer. Jasper didn't drink really, and I had never seen anyone order alcohol at this type of place. I started to panic, but tried to focus on the incredible food in front of me. After a bellyful of porky, doughy pillows, we went to the Museum of the Moving Image, and I felt the suicidal thoughts start to creep in. I had screwed everything up. Here I was in a cool, chic Queens museum, and all I wanted in life was unfettered access to another beer.

I headed over to a quiet corner and tried to compose myself. I found myself praying to God to help relieve me of this. We left the museum and went back to Jasper's apartment. The consensus was that everyone felt tired, so Jasper suggested takeout. My first opportunity to have a drink and he had ruined it. We ordered Thai food, and I excused myself to go to the bodega and get some soda. I came back with beer and tried to get the both of them to have one. They refused and the room was quiet. I wondered just how much of a secret my drinking problem really was.

The weeks that followed felt like more of the same. Wake up, spend time on the computer researching various story ideas, turn on *Sex and the City* and crack open the wine at 6 P.M., fall slowly into a blackout. Yunna was home most nights but I preferred drinking alone, with no one watching. My therapist with the kind eyes told me that I needed to start going back to AA or she could not treat me. She said that I was medicating with alcohol, and it was medically or clinically impossible to work through my grief while in an active stage of alcoholism. She suggested an outpatient facility, but I took a look at my bank account and knew that there were other, life-centric things like rent and groceries I had to use that money for.

The last day I drank was not like all the days that came before it. There was no blackout or shoving match or lost job. It was just the depression I felt that came sweepingly into focus *every single time* I was hungover. I knew that sobriety had worked for my dad, and yet I still felt unwilling to apply it to my own life. My brain shouted at me that he had *real* consequences as a result of his drinking. He was a junkie who left me and my twin in our snowsuits in a freezing cold car while he went to a crack house to get high. Having a morning shower beer was pathetic—JV shit—and I should just shut up and learn how to drink. But the other, more rational side of my brain understood that I was at the end of some sort of road and that I would lose whatever HBO project I had cooking if I continued to consume alcohol in the way that my genes wanted me to. I also often thought back to my sister dragging me into the shower. That is where my life was headed.

My other motivation felt even simpler. I wanted to honor my dad and live a life that he would be proud of, and I knew that I could not accomplish that if I continued drinking. I had to give it up. On August 23, 2015, my stepmom offered me a beer at dinner. I quietly said no then, as I did thousands of other times in small and big moments in the days and years that followed.

32

Resentments

"It's normal to lose a parent," Jill remarked to Meagan one afternoon as we headed into our first winter without him.

"Have you lost either of your parents?" Meagan replied, as carefully as she could.

"No," Jill admitted.

But I could understand the unsaid half of what Jill was saying. She and my dad were married for more than twenty years and considered each other their closest confidants. I have many memories of them dancing through the kitchen with the music cranked up way past the normal parent-friendly audio setting. Most often my view of them was sitting at the kitchen table side by side, reading the *Times* together. Both she and my dad were independent and stubborn, but they were each other's constant.

They were not people who included their children in their relationship. They had their own coded way of speaking to each other. Nicknames, media gossip—I was never sure what they were talking about. And they made little effort to change that when we would complain about it. Eventually we stopped when we realized that this was who they were: a couple devoted to each other who showed one another respect and love—a model I made a mental note to try to emulate someday.

Jill told me that the night before he died, she'd slept on the spare bed in the attic. She was sick with a nasty cold and didn't

want to pass along any germs before his panel the following evening. Her last night, another thing snatched away by circum-
stance.

Jill and I had never been close. She, who came into our lives
when Meagan and I were six, had been the designated discipli-
narian, always insisting on good manners and respect toward
our elders. But our relationship with her never went much beyond that. Never really softened. I was sure it was hard for her
then, as it was now. I could have used some softness, though.

It was November. The holidays would soon be here. I had
been actively trying to not think about Thanksgiving, my dad's
favorite. I remembered past Thanksgivings and cringed. I recalled 2013 as being a particularly hard year in our relationship.
I'd kept delaying, refusing to commit to any plan for the day of
feasting, and eventually got a furious call from Dad. Where was
I? Everyone was waiting for me. I threw some sweatpants on,
which I knew would piss him off, and headed to the dreaded
Port Authority.

My dad had always wanted his kids to be as excited about
Thanksgiving as he was. There was none of the annoyance of
gifts or reindeer that Christmas entailed. Turkey Day was just
about the turkey and us, and that was something he could certainly get down with. Every year he was responsible for the bird,
while Jill would handle most of the sides, except for the gravy.
My dad was a complete freak about gravy. He would labor in the
kitchen making his homemade savory concoction, tasting and
seasoning it until he declared perfection. When we were called
to the table for the meal, he would smile and ask people to taste
it. "Nothing is too good for my family," he would say as he
grinned toothily at us.

We were traditionalists and held hands and went around the
table to say what we were thankful for. Often, he discussed his
sobriety and his love of us, his girls. Work was rarely mentioned.

I can taste that gravy now. I have never attempted to re-create his magic.

On this day, with Thanksgiving a few weeks away, that magic was gone. I turned to Google for answers: "how to get through the holidays without murdering anyone." Hmm, grief seems to be missing in that Internet query. I add "grief." Whammo: "64 Tips for Coping with Grief During the Holidays." Sixty-four seemed an oddly specific number, but I figured I'd take each one I could get; however, "Lighting a candle and thinking 'nice' thoughts" about my dad sounded like a fast route to a revolver-in-mouth-type depression. I was looking for a more pragmatic approach, the advice the brunette best friend character in a movie would dispense: Stay off social media, eat whatever you want, and this sucks, and it should, because nothing a website or anyone else says can make him come back.

Meagan organized a group video chat to discuss how "we as a family" wanted to spend our first Turkey Day without him. She was always doing that, thinking about us as a unit instead of the fragmented individuals we had become. Jill had moved into a new, smaller house, and that might have been an option, but she wouldn't be there because she had to be in Tokyo for work. I was secretly relieved. I thought I would much rather scarf down bowls of green curry, alone, with *The Office* playing in the background, than try to get through this ludicrous holiday and all its trappings.

Meagan wouldn't have it. She suggested we three girls gather in Michigan because she had space and was willing to cook. Like a jerk, I automatically said, "Pass." Traveling during the holidays is such a nightmare. Never mind that she'd done it for the past ten years. Boston was brought up, as Madeline was there attending college. I said yes to Boston since it was closer than Michigan. "We can rent an Airbnb and cry together," I said.

Meagan got off the phone so quickly that I knew I should call her back. She picked up, and her voice was fractured and soft, like she'd been crying. I asked what was wrong, but I knew the answer.

"I just don't know what to say. No one is making an effort for us to be together. It's important that we stay connected. . . ."

Her voice trailed off but I knew what she was implying.

I nodded but said nothing.

At the end of the phone call, we agreed on Boston because it was near-ish to all of us. Our grandma, Jill's mom, who is also known as Grammy Diane, would fly out from Minnesota and be the stand-in for Jill. She is kind, sweet, and loves Elvis Presley. She is a young sort of grandma and a reassuring presence. Plus she always brings us candy. On this Thanksgiving, we chose gummy bears over turkey.

I felt a mixture of emotions about my stepmother as we headed into the holiday. I felt grateful that my little sister still had a parent, but I was unable to ask Jill to be mine. I'm not sure if she was ever fully my parent. I'm not sure if my dad ever allowed her to grow into that role. He was our mother and father; he wanted to be all things to us. Intellectually, I knew I was not a child. Still, I relished my anger over her absence, and that was both troubling and comforting. It wasn't that I wanted Jill to be there; I just felt comfortable being mad at her. Placing blame somewhere. It felt good to feel something other than sadness.

Jasper offered to drive me up to Boston. As we got in the car the air felt bitingly cold. I had underdressed as usual, and I cursed the whole Northeast as a region. Madeline's friends had agreed to let us stay at their apartment for one hundred bucks, but I'd been warned that it was a complete and total pit. The Airbnb idea had been nixed because we were all broke and there was no parent around to pay for it.

I was three months sober (again) at the time, and was craving a drink to take the edge off of what I could only imagine would be a disaster. When I arrived, the mood was pretty much dire. Meagan had been scrubbing the apartment for hours, as she wanted the place to be suitable for our grandma. Madeline was holed away in one of her friends' bedrooms, stricken with bronchitis or some other joy-suppressing ailment, but came out to survey the work being done and say hello. Jasper said hi to everyone and then gave me a quick hug goodbye as he headed out the door. I knew he was happy to return to his nondepressed family, which irritated me. I wished I could hide in his trunk and go back to the land of dumplings and plush red blankets. Instead I was stuck with two of the witches from *Macbeth*. I completed the set.

"Hey, do you want some help cleaning?" I offered unconvincingly.

"No, I'm fine. Almost done," Meagan responded quietly as she swept the remaining dust into the dustpan.

"It's a good thing Dad doesn't have to be here this year," I joked, trying to break the tension. She looked up, said nothing, and walked away.

Later we headed to a museum on the T, our grandma now with us. Jill hadn't called. The time difference was too much from Tokyo to Boston. There was a general uneasiness that permeated every discussion our little family had. We were outside our routine, and I was filled with resentments. I resented Jill for being gone, Meagan for forcing us to spend time together, my dad for dying, and Madeline for coughing all night long. I walked from room to room in the Isabella Stewart Gardner Museum, reading about the 1990 theft of the prized Rembrandt *Christ in the Storm, on the Sea of Galilee,* among others. I wondered who on earth had those paintings and what they'd done with them. Anything to take my mind off the present. Amid my reverie, I caught a glimpse of my sisters as we all walked toward the end of the exhibit. All I recall is liking the feeling of being lost in the art rather than in my own head.

At the end of the day, I crawled under the covers with my two sisters, uncomfortable, anxious, longing for my own bed. I've read that in grief, families come together or break at the seams. In that moment it felt obvious what sort we were.

That night, late into the wee hours, I asked Meagan about what Dad would have thought about our first holiday effort without him. I knew he would be beyond disappointed, maybe even furious with the results. But I couldn't seem to get any closer than I was, sharing a pillow. I watched the ceiling as I waited for Meagan to answer. We might have been alone as we worked our way through the night, but at least I could try to be as physically close as possible.

Trying to smile and get through our first Thanksgiving without him.

33

Sad Girl's Guide

"Woke up last nite thinking about you—
did you know you are always on my mind?"

Before my father's I had only witnessed death in disparate flashes, mostly through social media. A girl from high school was running in the park at exactly the wrong moment and part of an oak tree splintered off and hit her. She died instantly. My high school mourned her through a Facebook post, and it caught my attention. My mind recalled another death that made little sense. Outside the tutoring place where I worked, a girl named Michelle told me that her sister, a twin, had died speeding down a street in our town at one in the afternoon. The twins were identical, and I immediately imagined the parents looking at her, exactly the same as the child they had lost.

These disruptions in space and time rattled me. Why did these young women die? After college, the Facebook posts started coming every couple of months, notifications that one friend of mine or another had lost a parent or grandparent after a long illness. I melted into the pictures, looking at the toothy smiles of proud relatives no longer here. I scrolled my way through the tapestry of their relationship. The big moments that they'd been there for and would not be in the future. It shocked my system. Now it was my turn.

As a millennial, I tend to crowdsource everything. So why

not grief? I wrote to the three women I knew who had lost a parent, revealing that I had lost one, too, and asked a series of inane/oversimplified questions:

Were there any books or movies that helped you?
What was absolutely not helpful to you?
Did you gain weight? Did you lose weight?
How do I wake up in the morning and not feel insane? How do I work?
How do I cope (without using wine)?
How do I deal with the self-pitying thoughts that are on a loop in my brain?
How can I talk to my dad still?
Did writing help?
What do I do when I feel irrational rage when people are talking about their parents?
How do I communicate about it with people that I do not know?

My friend and fellow namesake Erin was the first to respond. Her words floored me. But first, a little about her: Erin is captivating in looks and in spirit. She is the former girlfriend of a boy I loved. She has dark, shiny brown hair with large oval brown eyes. Freckles line the top of her cheeks. She looks like an actress Warhol would have hung out with. Porcelain skin with a penetrating gaze. I felt immediately jealous as I secretly crawled through her digital existence. I heard that she could be mean and sharp. I met her and kept a distance, jealous but also intrigued.

A close friend of hers moved to the city, and I offered to take him out to a VICE party. I wore a black fitted dress with my jet-black hair, never making a move and understanding that I should not because I was likely to be rejected. I got a message from Erin, early the next day, saying I should stay away from her friends. We were so, so similar, it was painful. Years later, she apologized and asked for a meeting. The stars aligned and we saw each other for what we were, kindred spirits and drinking buddies. When I first got sober she supported the cause.

Her mother died in a personal tragedy (her story to tell, not mine) that I watched unfold through the Internet. I felt awful for Erin but didn't know what to do or say, so I said nothing. This was before my dad died, and I knew little about the etiquette of grief.

The next time I saw her, her skin was paler, almost translucent. Her face looked thinner. I asked her what the most difficult thing was. Zeroing in on the question made me feel stupid, but I could not speak the dreaded words "How are you doing?" She closed her eyes and said, "Everything." I nodded.

But when I needed her, after my father died, she was there. This is the response she sent me.

To: Erin Lee Carr
From: Erin C
Date: 02/24/2015
Subject: Sad Club

Have you ever read East of Eden? I think it's the first thing i read after losing my mom that really got close to me. For me, self-help books or books on grief don't get through to me. Maybe because they threaten to make your pain universal? You know? Like no one in the world feels exactly like you do right now, and although so many come close, you have to naturally find the stories that come to you, without coercion. Just pick up anything that piques your interest, through divine force it will have something in it for you. But omg I'm basic, because Wild made me sob uncontrollably. I think it's easy to relate to avoiding that pain and loss and what it will do to you. I think both you and I are the "type" to push those feelings as far back as we can . . . but it will destroy you. Gotta ride those waves up and down. Do not fight the weeping just yet. Let your body move through it.

You need to work at your own pace. I know it must be so difficult for you, being that he is so entwined with your work. You know how bummed he would be if this got in the way of your fucking master-piece though. Take all that work ethic he ingrained in you and do what you are meant to be doing. Get it girl, I know you will. But re-member if you need a personal day, you need a personal day. Just don't let those add up to weeks and then months. I am not con-cerned about your work. You will do great things. You are destined to.

Waking up is the worst part because you have to remind yourself. Rather, it's that mean self-sabotaging side of you that is hitting you with that as soon as you wake. The only thing that can really help this is to start thinking of everything you are grateful for when you feel hit down by his absence first thing. Hey, you are waking up, you are alive, you have a home, you have love, you are not hungry, you are incredibly taken care of by this universe. I know this is some new-agey shit, but it is completely true Erin. You will have to eventu-ally replace this grief with appreciation and understanding.

The wine is really difficult, because I want you to be able to have a glass, but at the same time i really don't. Keep going to your AA meetings. At all family functions I typically am the only one drinking, and my family watches me so closely because I mimic my mother. This past Christmas I didn't drink because it wasn't worth upsetting my family, because they are right to be concerned. Go to your meet-ings. I will be happy to join you again.

When i caught myself feeling bad for myself, i had to remember that I was so fucking lucky to have my mother at all. Fuck, even to have my mother into early adulthood IS FUCKING REMARKABLE in this world. Kids are orphaned everywhere without ever experiencing a drop of support or parental love. You know?

Literally none of my friends had lost a parent when my mom passed. It was/is so isolating and I would feel fucking LIVID when someone would complain about a parent or even talk about them at all. These situations are the ones where you have to be kinder than you feel. Be tender. Everyone will lose their parents, even though somehow we convince ourselves it will never happen. And like I said to you before, you are standing face-first with your nightmare. The other ones don't know it yet and have to subconsciously fear it until their time comes to say goodbye. Be tender Erin, it is not their fault and they don't have any idea yet.

I used my mouse to highlight all the words that she'd given me and create a new Google document. I thought for a moment and then typed in "Sad Girl's Guide" as the title in the upper left-hand corner. "Tender." It was not something I ever thought about. How to be kind when I only felt rage? Her words buoyed me and kept me afloat.

In addition to my new Google doc, I printed the email out and carefully hid the pages in the back section of my leather-enclosed notebook, the same notebook I'd taken to hear him talk on the night he died. It houses the last words I would hear him speak onstage. The next page contains my hastily scribbled notes for his funeral arrangements.

But even as I tried to process and reconcile my grief, the truth remained that I felt deeply envious of anyone who still had parents. It was the kind of irrational emotion that made me slam down my computer screen, walk away mid-conversation, and close myself off in my room. It's like a blindfold is removed after the death of your parent; you no longer view the world as open.

I abhorred the big holidays and the family portraits, my eyes narrowing whenever I came into close physical or digital contact. This quiet fury was not short-lived. Even a year later, I surprised myself with my inability to exist around women and their fathers. An image of my friend Sam and her smiling dad popped up onscreen. She's the kind of cool, aloof girl with bangs that I always wanted to be. Skinny long legs without trying, with a freelance filmmaking career that she mostly liked. The photos burned me up—the dad and daughter duo just looked so happy in the woods, enjoying each other's company. I clicked on the upper right-hand tab and saw UNFOLLOW SAM. I paused for a second, deliberating whether or not I should excommunicate her from my digital life just for the sin of having a father. I clicked on UNFOLLOW as I lied to myself with the pretense of practicing self-care. The truth was that it was too painful to bear witness to the hallmark moments I no longer had access to.

This is what they don't discuss with you after loss. The rage that bubbles up inside you, creating further divisions in your already fractured self. Loss turned me into someone who had a hard time functioning around other family units. I asked my sister if she felt the same way.

"Depends on the day, but mostly I just grin and bear it."

I marveled at her ability to extend beyond her comfort zone, refusing to let grief dictate how she related to the people around her. I vowed, like most days, to try to be more like my wombmate.

I headed over to my friend Zoe's apartment with a bag full of yarn—I'd decided I would like to take up knitting. I used to see people doing it all the time in church basements, and I needed something to do with my hands. We clicked PAUSE on the high-pitched voice squawking at us from the YouTube knitting tutorial and took a brownie break. She asked if I'd reached out to Sam. I shook my head dismissively. "Nah, I haven't talked to her in ages. She barely remembers me." Zoe sensed that information was missing and told me that Sam's dad had died unexpectedly after a brain operation. I instantly felt hideous for blocking her. He'd been having an operation and she'd wanted him to feel supported, hence all the pictures.

I texted Sam immediately and was met with zero response. I knew firsthand the flurry of messages that come after a big-deal loss. I waited patiently for a reply, which came the next day. She described the black hole her brain was in, and I instantly exhaled, feeling her grief viscerally. I attempted to be helpful and gave her tips on getting through the next couple of weeks and mentioned my Google document surrounding the topic of loss. She perked up and asked to see it. I told her I would answer my own questions and send it over. I reminded her it was okay to not be okay, and with that she moved toward the business of death.

To: Sam M
From: Erin Lee Carr
Date: 04/02/2016
Subject: SGC

Sam,

It's really the worst. Here are my answers to my own questions:

On books/movies—I tried reading grief books at first and just found them to be so blasé and unmanageable. Now finally able to explore the space i.e. Meghan O'Rourke, Wild, internet pieces. Silly but lite—

Radical Self Love. Movies: I can't stand sad movies, or dramas actually. I need humor in my life at the end of the day. I turn on Gilmore
Girls, Sex and the City, 30 Rock. Women being funny and complicated at the same time.

On helpful/not helpful—lost a fair amount of friends. I realized I was
a person who had a shit ton of acquaintances. I decided I want to
pick 10 people and work on my relationships with those people. I
want to have fun dates where we do/make things. I also want to pri-
oritize people who had gone through the same sort of loss as they
are easier to relate to.

On weight—I coped with food. I gained 15 pounds. I ate mac n'
cheese whenever I wanted. Oh and the pure magic that is double
stuff Oreos. I was scared when I looked at myself in pictures in July,
my twin tried to talk to me about it as gently as she could. I put myself on a diet in August and lost 10 pounds and it was a ton of work. I
am trying to get into working out, it's just so hard for me.

On waking up—Put something next to your bed that makes you
smile. I got a fancy coffee maker that made it nice to wake up to. And
flowers/plants . . . important for your eyes and brain to be near in my
experience. I try to write a daily gratitude list. I let myself feel sad and
cry if I need to.

On work—it was really hard at first. I would literally mentally blackout and not be able to focus. I took myself home the rest of the day if
that was happening. Around six months, I started putting myself
wholly into work and it made my life more manageable. Instead of
talking about how sad I was I could talk about the work that I was
doing. HBO greenlit me to direct a movie, I was hired to develop a
feature about the global arms industry and I was mentoring at CUNY.
It was a hustle and I felt so tired at the end of the day. I think my anx-
iety/stress spiked during that time but keeping busy was important
for me.

On wine—total non-starter due to my genetic predisposition. I used wine and it used me back. Awful. Had to give up. I drank on the six months anniversary and cried for like six hours straight. Felt totally gothic. I had my last drink August 23, 2015. I have been sober ever since.

On what to tell myself—I was gifted with a wonderful dad who told me over and over how much he loved me. So many people do not get that. Yes, we want more time but I, right now at this moment feel gratitude for what I had. Also: people die in wars and tragic horrifying accidents. My dad was not healthy, he drank and drugged for years, got sober but then smoked ~48 cigarettes a day. He also died the way he would have wanted, not a struggle or a diminishment of his mental facilities. He died with grace and dignity and on top of his game, at the *Times,* a place he adored. Sort of a mic drop, really.

On writing—it helps me. It's painful, earnest work. I think he would approve.

On other humans and their parents—I draw very strict boundaries as we discussed. I don't want to hear about your parents unless I ask. I reserve the right to leave the room. I feel triggered around holidays. I don't know if I will always be able to be direct. It feels like people are giving me a "pass" right now but that won't hold up forever. I feel concerned about that but try not to worry.

Best, E

I reviewed my responses. They were brusque and yet honest. In this moment, I felt the uniqueness of the situation drift away from me. I was one of many, trying to determine the next right step. I knew that attempting to help other people was meaningful work, and I would continue as best as I could muster. No more unfollowing.

34

A Glacier First Melts at the Edges

My dad was asked by the Alaska Press Club to speak at their 2015 annual conference, discussing reporting and the civic good it presents. Sadly, he didn't live long enough to attend the gig. The next year the organization asked me to speak about my process of filmmaking. While I had reservations—would they think I was a cheap imitation of the real thing?—I said yes. He would have wanted me to, right?

I couldn't email him about the invitation to go to Alaska. He was gone. Also gone were our phone calls, Gchats, the everuseful feedback, and the plotting of our next moves.

I insisted on heading to the airport from Jasper's house rather than my apartment because traveling made me anxious, and I liked to be by our dog Gary's side as long as possible. Gary knew how to spoon and was just about the best thing I had going on in my life. He eyed me dolefully, knowing that the suitcase meant the lady who sneaked him human food was going somewhere. I asked Jasper if I could practice my talk in front of him. He was sitting at his computer, lost in the AV Club, and heard me but only slightly.

"Um, yeah. I am sure it'll be great, babe."

This was one of many presentations or meetings that I sought his advice on. For me as a freelancer, it was one meeting after another, with many keeping me up at night. My boyfriend carried a lot of the weight, especially now that my dad was gone. It's uncomfortable, but sometimes necessary, how we force people in our lives to occupy certain roles. I was frustrated to not even get a glance from him as I spoke; his eyes were glued to the computer screen.

I walked into the bathroom and gently closed the door. I leaned in, putting my hands on the porcelain sink. I stared at myself. I thought I looked older than twenty-eight. My hair was pulled back into a ponytail, and freckles lined my face even though the sun hadn't come out yet. It was April, and it had been what seemed like a very long winter. My face looked puffy, and I had the requisite circles of a workaholic underneath my eyes. I splashed cold water on my face and took a deep breath. I said to myself, loudly: *You will be great.*

The flight was literally across the entire continent, but I started to feel the burn at hour two. I watched movies, wrote a proposal, outlined my next shoot, and still had eight hours to kill. I am rarely alone with my thoughts for this long. They aren't always the best company.

I finally reached Anchorage, feeling a fresh wave of excitement as I headed over to pick up my rental car. I could say or do whatever I wanted for the next twenty-four hours before my talk. I headed toward the Bubbly Mermaid, a champagne and oyster bar off the main strip. No white wine for me, I told the kind and curvaceous waitress. I ordered enough oysters to feed three, plus some pâté, and I felt somewhat like an adult. I realized I was mimicking behavior that I'd observed in my dad. You fly somewhere, ask a local for the best food shack, and overspend on food because you are not buying booze. I even toted my Harry Potter book with me to add to my big-kid status. I thought momentarily about ordering a glass of champagne. *No one would know,* a mischievous voice inside my head commented. I swatted the thought away. I'd only been sober this time for six months, but I wanted to keep it that way.

I left the restaurant full of oysters and received a call from an unknown number. In my line of work, that typically meant I was about to talk to someone in a prison. My heart picked up its pace as I timidly said "Hello." I spoke with a young man who had been accused of raping a sixteen-year-old at an elite boarding school. The prosecutor said that he'd lured her via the school intranet and assaulted her and bragged about it to his friends. I had read through hundreds of his chats, and I knew many secrets about him, and yet here he was on the phone, calling me Ms. Carr and asking me about myself. He was awaiting sentencing after a guilty verdict and was very careful not to say anything that would incriminate him, so he couldn't say much. I hung up and felt my life moving away from my dad's death and into work that scared me. He would approve.

Over the next couple of days, I spoke to students and drank shitty coffee that somehow tasted fine in one of the truly most spectacular places on earth. Speakers at the conference knew my dad, and quickly said, "Sorry for your loss," before moving on to the next topic. I found that the righteous anger that had been with me the first year had started to leave me and these conversations. I liked when people mentioned him now. He was in their thoughts just as he was in mine. I felt kinship with the other women and men who had been asked to speak. There was Zoe, a fierce and loud radio reporter from a well-known program; Bob, a blowhard from that same radio organization; and a young man named Bryan who spent time analyzing all the folks who read *The Washington Post.* I felt instantly crushy toward Bryan, but the feeling retreated as he gave me tips on how to successfully move in with a significant other.

For one night, we were invited to a fancy, secluded resort in Seward. The drive there was dangerous because I was alone and gawking at the sights around me, instead of paying attention to the winding road ahead. When we arrived, we all grabbed drinks. I felt like I was fresh out of elementary school when I ordered a Shirley Temple with extra cherries, like my former self had been exposed as someone who could not handle her liquor. We talked about the start of the year, hard work, and loss. David Bowie had died, and this little group of artists talked it through. I felt myself harden when Zoe talked about the pain of losing a man like Bowie. "What right do we have to mourn a man we never knew?" I wondered out loud.

I explained that it was hard to hear that sort of thing when you have recently lost a parent. Zoe swiveled to face me and whispered, "Wait, your dad was David Carr?"

I looked down and blushed. "Yes."

She recounted reading *The Night of the Gun,* listening to his Terry Gross interview, and seeking comfort in his words after her mother died. It became one of many instances in which an individual would hold my hand and say how much he had meant to them. I started to understand the spasm of grief. Once someone close to you dies, you feel loss more plainly, as it is a part of your everyday experience. It feels crushing as the wave hits you, but then you can see the tide begin to drift in and out again after the storm.

The day before I was scheduled to go home, I decided to venture to a glacier to see what the fuss was all about. It was raining outside, but luckily I had a waterproof coat from Costco that my always practical sister Meagan had gifted me. A sign commanded me to LOOK OUT FOR BEARS. I resisted the impulse to put in my white earbuds, and instead embraced the sound of the crunch of rocks and pebbles under my feet in the otherwise silent setting. The landscape was a watercolor of brown, gray, and white. Snow blanketed every mountaintop, and for the first time in a long while, I let go of what was happening that week, even that day. I focused on my breath, in that minute, and the world that I was surrounded by. I took a picture to remember the moment, but I knew it would have been better to leave it—to become untethered to the digital rope that binds me. I put my phone away after I took this photo, knowing that experiences like this were rare and best not seen through a screen.

I walked down the path deeper into the park and saw the peak from far off. Not knowing the proper etiquette, I climbed on top of the snow-covered glacier and took out a carefully folded piece of paper from my pocket. I read it out loud.

I try to say "I love you" every day to him. Just in case he is in a place quiet enough to hear it. The skeptic in me doubts that he listens, but still I do it. I don't have concrete evidence that life exists beyond death, but I know I felt connected to him that day. I felt small and large all at once on the frozen wave. The glacier moves so slowly that the movement is impossible to register.

Listen when you enter a room.

Don't buy into your myth.

Don't be the first one to talk, but if you do talk first, say something smart.

Speak and then stop; don't stutter or mumble; be strong in what you have to say.

Be defiant.

You have to work the phones. Call people. Don't rely on emails.

Ask questions but ask the right questions.

Ask people what mistakes they've made so you can get their shortcuts.

Know when enough is enough.

Make eye contact with as many people as possible.

Don't be in shitty relationships because you are tired of being alone.

Be grateful for the things you have in this life. You are lucky.

Practice patience even though it's one of the hardest things to master.

Failure is a part of the process, maybe the most important part.

Alcohol is not a necessary component of life.

Street hotdogs are not your friend.

Remind yourself that nobody said this would be easy.

If more negative things come out of your mouth than positive, then Houston, we have a problem.

We contain multitudes.

Always love (See band: Nada Surf).

Have a dance move and *don't be afraid* to rock it.

Don't go home just because you are tired.

Don't take credit for work that is not yours. If your boss does this, take note.

Be generous with praise and be specific in that praise: "That line was killer."

Cats are terrible; they poop in your house.

Say what you mean and mean what you say.

Do the next right thing.

Our dogs are us. Only cuter.

And finally:

You are loved and you belong to me, the world, and yourself.

BOOKS I READ WHILE WRITING THIS BOOK

The Night of the Gun: A Reporter Investigates the Darkest Story of His Life—His Own by David Carr

The Art of Memoir by Mary Karr

The Year of Magical Thinking by Joan Didion

The Gilded Razor: A Memoir by Sam Lansky

On Writing: A Memoir of the Craft by Stephen King

*Weird in a World That's Not: A Career Guide for Misfits, F*ckups, and Failures* by Jennifer Romolini

Handling the Truth: On the Writing of Memoir by Beth Kephart

The Men in My Life: A Memoir of Love and Art in 1950s Manhattan by Patricia Bosworth

Hunger: A Memoir of (My) Body by Roxane Gay

Girl Walks Out of a Bar: A Memoir by Lisa F. Smith

How to Murder Your Life: A Memoir by Cat Marnell

Kids These Days: Human Capital and the Making of Millennials by Malcolm Harris

You Don't Look Your Age . . . and Other Fairy Tales by Sheila Nevins

The Long Goodbye: A Memoir by Meghan O'Rourke

M Train by Patti Smith

Ninety Days: A Memoir of Recovery by Bill Clegg

Five Men Who Broke My Heart: A Memoir by Susan Shapiro

It's Okay to Laugh (Crying Is Cool Too) by Nora McInerny Purmort

Daily Rituals: How Artists Work by Mason Currey

Empty Mansions: The Mysterious Life of Huguette Clark and the Spending of a Great American Fortune by Bill Dedman and Paul Clark Newell, Jr.

Shrill: Notes from a Loud Woman by Lindy West

Talking as Fast as I Can: From "Gilmore Girls" to "Gilmore Girls" (And Everything in Between) by Lauren Graham

Down City: A Daughter's Story of Love, Memory, and Murder by Leah Carroll

Grit: The Power of Passion and Perseverance by Angela Duckworth

We Are Never Meeting in Real Life: Essays by Samantha Irby

Mental: Lithium, Love, and Losing My Mind by Jaime Lowe

ACKNOWLEDGMENTS

I could not and would not have written this without you, Dad. Your work, emails, and Gchats have sustained me and will continue to do so.

To my smart, sharp, and yet so kind editor, Pamela Cannon: You saw something in that *Medium* piece that started this journey. I learned so much from working on this with you. I think my dad would have liked your edits.

I need to do a heartfelt and perhaps-too-loud clap for the instantly winning and charming Meg Thompson. You made me believe I could do this, and it was your early line edits that got me through. An additional heartfelt thank-you to Kiele Raymond at Thompson Literary Agency who helped in countless ways. Thank you for your time and thoughtfulness regarding this manuscript.

To Jill: I love you.

To Maddie: There is no one like you.

To Meagan: This book was written for you. We have had quite a life.

To Mom: I know this is hard; thank you for understanding.

To Derek Stump: Thank you for your help with the *Medium* piece and the early drafts of these chapters. I am excited to read your book one day.

To William Patrick: You, too, have a myth.

To Jessica Nordell: Your notes meant the world to me.

To Leah Carroll: I hung up your early encouragement on my wall.

To the Carr family: John, Joe, Missy, Lisa, and Jim.

Ta-Nehisi Coates, Lena Dunham, A. O. Scott.

Sheila Nevins and Sara Bernstein. Docuwitches for life!

Andrew Rossi: I love making movies with you and our team/ family. You teach me how to be a better journalist, director, and friend.

Moving pictures: Andrew Coffman, Bryan Sarkinen, Alison Byrne, Ian Hultquist, Kate Novack, Neil Cohen, Sarah Gibson, Jen Maylack, Alex Gibney, Rob Booth, Shane Sigler, Richard Levengood, Stacey Offman, Brian McGinn, Janet Pierson, Bethany Haynes.

Jasper Lin, Erin Tonken, Diana Lauren Gonzalez-Morett, Jeremy Barr, Zoe Miller, Tim Cheng, Macaela Sears, Hamilton Nolan, Matt Yoka, Patricia Bosworth, Justin Reed, Kathleen Flood, Jake Grupp, Sophie Saint Thomas, Rhana Natour, Bruce Orwall, Anna Reinhart, Vicki Davis, Amy Emmerich, Heather McCabe, Chris Russo, Elise Furer, Solange Lasso, Katie Drummond, Maxine Presto, Malcolm Harris, Katherine Lanpher, Lam Thuy Vo, Ariella Abuaf, Cora Engelbrecht, Michael Borrelli, Mel Clark, Faith Gaskins, Liz Horowitz, Jeff Aldrich, Danielle Neftin, John Otis, Kenyatta Matthews, Yana Collins Lehman, and Jenna Wortham.

Ballantine Books, Penguin Random House, *Medium*.

To anyone who has ever agreed to sit down for an interview with me. I know what it feels like now.

To Yunna, my muse and cheerleader: You are one of the smartest, most empathic people I know. You root for others and that is a rarity. I root for you, today and always. Plus you got me to love beets!

YOU (for reading this; now go write someone you love an email).

ABOUT THE AUTHOR

Erin Lee Carr is a director, producer, and writer based in New York City. Named one of the "30 Under 30" most influential people in media by *Forbes,* Carr most recently directed *At the Heart of Gold,* about the USA Gymnastics scandal, and *I Love You, Now Die,* about the Michelle Carter murder-by-texting trial, both for HBO. She also directed "Drug Short," an episode of Netflix's critically acclaimed series *Dirty Money. All That You Leave Behind* is her debut book. See lives in New York City, where she enjoys petting dogs on the street.

erinleecarr.com
Twitter: @erinleecarr
Instagram: @erinleecarr

ABOUT THE TYPE

This book was set in Minion, a 1990 Adobe Originals typeface by Robert Slimbach. Minion is inspired by classical, old-style typefaces of the late Renaissance, a period of elegant and beautiful type designs. Created primarily for text setting, Minion combines the aesthetic and functional qualities that make text type highly readable with the versatility of digital technology.